PIGLET'S PROCESS

PROCESS THEOLOGY FOR ALL GOD'S CHILDREN

BRUCE G. EPPERLY

Energion Publications
Gonzalez, Florida
2019

Cover Design: Henry E. Neufeld
Cover Image: Adobe Stock # 31317579

ISBN: 978-1-63199-728-0
eISBN: 978-1-63199-730-3

Library of Congress Control Number: 2019954488

Energion Publications
PO Box 841
Gonzalez, FL 32560
https://energion.com
pubs@energion.com

For Jack and James, my little grandchildren;
the children of the world; and the child in each of us, that we
may flourish and live joyfully on this good Earth. May your
imaginations be free of fear and full of possibility.

TABLE OF CONTENTS

A Journey Through the 100 Aker Wood

*In the middle of the journey of our life, I came to myself, in
a dark wood, where the direct way was lost. It is a hard thing to
speak of, how wild, harsh and impenetrable that wood was, so
that thinking of it recreates the fear. It is scarcely less bitter than
death: but, in order to tell of the good that I found there, I must
tell of the other things I saw there.*

This confession begins Dante Alighieri's *Divine Comedy*. Citing Dante seems like a strange way to embark on a book on Piglet, one of the heroes of A.A. Milne's children's classic *Winnie the Pooh*. What does a Very Small Animal have to do with a middle-aged man's fears of becoming irreparably lost in a dark wood? What does the innocence of the 100 Aker Wood have to do with anxieties aroused by enveloping darkness?[1]

The 100 Aker Wood is heaven on earth, the peaceable realm, dreamed of by prophet and political reformer, and the gentle place where children can stretch their imaginations. The characters of the 100 Aker Wood are good-hearted and intend the best, despite some occasional kerfuffles resulting from foolish decision-making or limited viewpoints. In the Wood, there is always a happy ending and a Bear and a boy can always meander in quiet woodlands, regardless of how old that child grows to be. Yet even in the best of circumstances, a Very Small Animal can feel anxious and on occasion stray off the right path and wander how he or she will get

---

1   Throughout the Winnie the Pooh books, A.A. Milne takes liberties
with spelling. These creative variations emerged from his observations
of his son Christopher's first attempts at spelling. If you have a copy
of the Pooh books nearby, you might skim it to see Milne's creative
appropriation of his son's youthful spelling.

home. Outside the Wood, there is the adult world of calculation and conflict, and the decisions of our leaders routinely put the Earth and the lives of our children and grandchildren in peril.

Books for children often emerge from adult imaginations and reflect the storyteller's hopes and fears. Those who read children's texts to their children and grandchildren find themselves straddling the worlds of innocence and experience, delighting in the naivete of the residents of the 100 Aker Wood but also bringing their own adult ruminations to the story. Written in the wake of World War I, A.A. Milne knew the atrocities of "the war to end all wars" and mourned the passing of a generation of England's finest young men. Perhaps Winnie the Pooh and Piglet emerged from the desire to escape the grief of the previous decade as well as to provide an entertaining vision of alternative reality, a world without hatred and violence, a community where friendship trumped alienation.

As I write these words, many Americans believe that our nation and world is lost in a dark wood with no direct way home. Fantasy has replaced factuality in politics and governmental decision-making, emotion has eclipsed reason, self-interest has superseded the quest for the common good, and leaders boast of the virtues of ignorance, all the while promising that they alone can save our nation. Across the globe from the Wood and Cape Cod where my grandchildren and I live, parents in Iraq and Syria shield their children from rocket attacks.   In urban America, mothers mourn the death of their children on city streets and toddlers are separated from the parents. Just beyond the Wood, national leaders and business moguls choose short term profits, pyrrhic political victories, and glamourous photo shoots over preservation of the planet.

Our earth is a glorious place, dazzling in its beauty, and yet we are often more anxious than amazed at we ponder the future of our planet. Saviors emerge in the body politic stoking our fears and then promising to solve all our problems.

Now more than ever we need the wisdom of the 100 Aker Wood. We need the wisdom of simple and good-hearted stuffed toys to help us find our way through the dark wood and reveal the foolishness of the powerful and wealthy. We need the harmony of the Wood to remind us of the beauty of diversity. The emperors have no clothes and the rich and power have lost their reason. That's clear to perceptive young children and to Eeyore and to Piglet as well.

In the dark wood, we need to return to the simple Gospel message, spoken by Jesus and echoing in the Wood: life is beautiful, there is enough for everyone, and we can wake up to a Graceful Providence that embraces all of us and gives us the inspiration and energy to take a new path, a path of justice, peace, and beauty. We need glimmers of light and rays of hope provided by simple, but profound stories, of forest animals and their human friend.

Piglet is a Small and Anxious animal and sometimes he has good reason to be afraid, especially as he imagines the mythical Heffalump and Woozle. In the dark wood of our lives, we may feel small and anxious as well as shadows fall on our fragile democracy and equally fragile planet. The personal and corporate challenges we face threaten overwhelm us; they are so large and we are so small. Yet, Piglet, unlike many of us, embraces his fear and discovers an inner courage that makes him a hero and model for us as we work up the courage to face the challenges of our time.

This book is about theology, and, in particular, process theology. These days, a good dose of healthy theology, a life-supporting vision of reality, to guide our decision-making is more important than ever. To many adults, theology is about as irrelevant as a children's book to the challenges of our time. But, the apparent fragility of imagination, presenting us with alternatives to the machinations of politicians is the only thing that can save us from fear and hopelessness. We need light-bearing visions of God and the world to illumine our path and banish the shadows of fear.

Theology is about thinking great thoughts and looking at the big picture rather than obsessing on the quick fix or short-term profit. Perhaps, now more than any time since World War II we need creative and life-transforming theological reflection, especially when televangelists and preachers have sold out the way of Jesus for a few crumbs at Caesar's table. We need good theology, easily understood and honest, to help us find our way through the Wood. Good theology shines a spotlight on our way, shapes our character, and gives us a framework for interpreting the apparent chaos of daily life. Good theology reminds us that a Gentle Providence guides our days, just as Providence inspires Piglet to give up his home for the good of another and to do what he had previously thought impossible to save his friends. We are, as the first followers of Jesus were called, "people of the Way," and the way we seek leads to abundant life for everyone, not just a select few.

This book is an interpretation of process theology through the life and encounters of Piglet. But, this dialogue with a stuffed pig is also a reflection on my adventures as a pastor, professor, teacher, parent, grandparent, friend, and citizen. This book gives homage to my teachers, John Cobb, David Griffin, Richard Keady, Marie Fox, and Bernard Loomer, who first introduced me to imaginative vision of process theology. It honors my dear friend Wendy Govier, not much bigger than Piglet herself, whose four-decade friendship was one of the greatest gifts of my life. Though they won't understand them yet, these words are also intended to inspire my two grandchildren, Jack and James, and to inspire adults to protect the innocence of children everywhere, including children we will never meet, from all that would harm them — the greed of political and business leaders, the violence of arms merchants and despots, the apathy of disinterested adults, our fear of pilgrims from other lands, and temptations of greed and consumerism. We are entering a dark wood, as Dante says, and we need a child — the child in us and his or her stuffed animal companions — to show us the way forward.

This book is a call to let the children play and to bless them as Jesus did so that their days might be long and healthy and full of joy on this good Earth. It is a call for every nation to put children, and our fragile blue-green planet, first and to ask before every decision, "How will this shape the lives children yet to be born as far in the future of seven generations from now?" Beyond responding to immediate issues of care, safety, and employment, this is the most important question we and our leaders must face. It is also a challenge to every adult to pay attention to the children in their lives and to rediscover and find healing for the anxious and playful child within. The fragility of the environment and social order reminds us to put prophets ahead of profits, and place planetary well-being ahead of short term economic or political gain. We need a place like the 100 Aker Wood to return for refreshment and to nourish our own imaginations so that we might discover large and life-affirming alternatives to the small, self-interested images proliferating in the media and the halls of prosperity and power.

Theology can change lives. Bad theology leads to violence and planetary destruction. We see this in the news every day — in the acts of "religious" terrorists who believe that murder and intolerance are blessed by God or worshippers of power who identify Jesus' movement with the bloviations of polarizing politicians. In contrast, healthy theology gives birth to hospitality and earth care. Imaging a God whose power is found in love will change us and our world.

We become like the gods we follow, and now more than ever we need a god — the True God, whose reality we can never fully describe — who inspires us to loving kindness, compassion, forgiveness, and care for the earth. We need an image of God who blesses little children, nurtures our highest aspirations, unites rather than divides the human race, and inspires us to claim our vocation as healers of this good Earth. This is the God, whose footsteps we glimpse in the 100 Aker Wood and the words of process theologians. In woodlands and seashores, our hearts awaken once more to love and our spirits to beauty. A little child can lead us. A Small Animal can guide us.

Sing ho for Piglet! Sing ho for Pooh! Sing ho for process theology! Sing ho for Jesus! Sing ho for love! Sing ho for every child!

EVERYDAY
ADVENTURES

Pooh and Piglet walked home thoughtfully together in the golden evening and for a long time they were silent.

"When you wake up in the morning, Pooh," said Piglet at last," what's the first thing you say to yourself?"

"What's for breakfast," said Pooh. "What you do you say, Piglet?

"I say, I wonder what's going to happen exciting today?" said Piglet. Pooh nodded thoughtfully. "It's the same thing," he said.[2]

"I wonder what's going to happen exciting today?" That's how Piglet begins each day, anticipating excitement even on the most ordinary day. Excitement is a way of life, and an adventurous approach to each day's beginning. We can be filled with excitement and amazement even in challenging times. We can ask ourselves, "What is the Great Work life calls us to today?"

Typically, we don't expect anything extraordinary to happen when we wake up in the morning and ponder the day ahead. Still, we may ask ourselves, "On an ordinary day, like today, how could anything exciting happen? If it did happen, would we notice it? Or would we simply pass by, oblivious to countless miracles strewn along our daily peregrinations? Would we be so caught up in adult illusions — the desire for power and security — that we miss beauty all around us? Would we think our projects so important that a Small Animal and a Pudgy Bear are of no consequence?" Then,

---

2   A.A. Milne, *The World of Winnie the Pooh* (New York: Penguin Books, 1985), 168.

we hear a little voice, whispering, "Hey, let's go on an expotition!" and off we go on an unexpected and holy adventure.

Excitement and wonder can happen any moment of the day, for those who senses are trained for adventure. Just this morning, as I drove my eight year old grandson to school, I was astounded as he wondered out loud, "I can't believe that I wasn't alive before I was born." To an adult who's listening, a young child's query uncovers the great mystery of the universe, the ultimate source of philosophy and religion, "Why is there something rather than nothing? Or, more particularly, why is there *this* something — this *me*, the one asking the question — and what was I before I came to be born here on planet earth?"

A few days earlier, his younger brother, age six, stumped me with his own questions, "How big is Jesus' heart? Is Jesus in my heart? Is Jesus in everybody's heart?" Tucked away in a small child's questions are precursors to erudite ruminations related to the scope of revelation and salvation, about whether Jesus inspires everyone or just the fortunate few who recite the right words and practice the right rituals. A child's innocent questions confound those who would separate the world into saved and unsaved, us and them, and faithful and infidel. A child's boundless imagination astounds and reveals the illusions of the religious and political elite who confine truth to a particular holy book, ritual, doctrine, or nation.

My grandchildren's questions remind me of my first theological queries. I recall at age five, spending a few days with a pious Baptist lady who was given the task of caring for my brother and me while my parents were at church convention. This pious lady Mrs. Orr had a dog named "Taffy," with whom I fell in love in the way that only a young child can experience a companion animal. I'd never had a dog as a companion and I was completely smitten by Taffy as we played for hours in Mrs. Orr's backyard. Being a pious Baptist boy myself, accustomed to revival meetings, altar calls, and confessions of faith, I asked this saint of the church, "Will Taffy go to heaven?" She looked at me strangely, pursed her lips in way adults do when they believe a child has done or said something out of line, or made a bad smell, and responded brusquely, "You'll have to talk with your father. He'll tell you that only humans go to heaven and that Jesus died to save us from our sins. Animals really don't matter to God."

At that moment, I became a theologian — albeit a *padawan* or novice, theologian, to use the language of Star Wars — who felt dissonance between my love for Taffy and Mrs. Orr's disdain for my concern for Taffy's soul. Deep down, I was hurt by her condescension, and although I did not challenge Mrs. Orr's theology at the time, that apparently chance but more likely providential encounter was a turning point in my own spiritual journey as the edifice of conservative Christianity of my childhood began to crumble. I wondered silently: "If God doesn't love Taffy, whom does God love, then? Doesn't God care about dogs and cats and whales, too? If God doesn't love Taffy, does God really love me?" Or, as my oldest grandson once asked, "Does God love sharks?"

Mrs. Orr's theology may have suited her, but it was far too small for me. It lacked stature and imagination. It excluded dogs and eagles, whales and chimpanzees, unbelievers and skeptics, and stuffed bears and their porcine companions! It enshrined a world view that sacrifices sacred grounds for oil pipelines, and aquafers and endangered species to pad our bank accounts and satisfy our consumerist whims.

The questions our children ask are entry ways to excitement and adventure. Rabbi Abraham Joshua Heschel once noted that the experience of radical amazement was at the heart of the spiritual journey. Without wonder and amazement, we can't really be religious, Heschel asserted. We live in an enchanted world in which burning bushes are everywhere, ready to speak to us, as they did to Moses, but we often have better things to do than seek guidance from a smoldering plant.

A little child will lead them, so says scripture. The child in ourselves, transfixed by a silver moon or the cry of an owl will guide our paths toward God. As we will discover in the pages ahead, meandering Pooh Bear and ambivalent Piglet may lead jaded adults like us on a holy adventure as well.

The Advent of Theology. As I pen these words, it is late November and the Advent season has just begun. In this first season of the Christian year, lasting just four weeks before Christmas, the watch words are "wake up," "turn around," "the whole world is bursting forth in beauty, don't miss it." The Expected One, the child whose birth will change the world, is on the horizon, coming where and when we least expect it. Look out, this child's birth counsels, you may be on an adventure and not know it! Yet! There may be a pattern in the events of your life — a gentle providence — to help you find your way and you haven't yet discovered it. Yet! Whether or not you are aware of it, the moment you awakened this morning and indeed, throughout the night as you slept, you have been a participant in a holy adventure, and you might not even know it — Yet!

As we meander through the 100 Aker Wood or our own neighborhood, we may discover that we live in a world chock-full with beauty. In the course of our quotidian activities, we may realize that no two moments are the same and every moment can become a portal into divinity.

Today can be a day of adventure and excitement. It certainly is in that imaginary Eden — the 100 Aker Wood — where Piglet and his companions spend their days. In the course of any day, adventure is always around the corner: Piglet and his friends can go on an Expotition to the North Pole, get stranded in a flood, celebrate a friend's birthday, go hunting for a Heffalump and nearly catch a Woozle, get lost in the woods and their way home lured by the scent of honey, and perform unexpected acts of heroism. That's the story of Piglet, a Small and Anxious Animal, an often-reluctant adventurer, who goes forth toward new horizons despite his initial misgivings. Always on the edge of adventure — inviting and frightening as the next adventure may be to him — little Piglet awakens the ambivalent and yet open-hearted adventurer in us!

Little Piglet and his woodland companions remind us that as in control of our lives as we believe ourselves to be, our lives are adventurous as well. We are not only part of a daily and lifetime adventure, but also a national, planetary, and cosmic adventure. "Wow!" is the only appropriate response to a sunrise or to images of our immune system or the Milky Way. "Hallelujah" is the only proper response to a child playing with a puppy dog, an osprey feathering its nest, or a Right While caring for its calf.

Carl Sagan describes his amazement as he sees an image of the Earth's journey through the Milky Way through the lens of the Voyager I spacecraft:

> *Look again at that dot. That's here. That's home. That's us. On it everyone you love, everyone you know, everyone you ever heard of, every human being who ever was, lived out their lives. The aggregate of our joy and suffering, thousands of confident religions, ideologies, and economic doctrines, every hunter and forager, every hero and coward, every creator and destroyer of civilization, every king and peasant, every young couple in love, every mother and father, hopeful child, inventor and explorer, every teacher of morals, every corrupt politician, every "superstar," every "supreme leader," every saint and sinner in the history of our species lived there — on a mote of dust suspended in a sunbeam.*

> *The Earth is a very small stage in a vast cosmic arena. Think of the rivers of blood spilled by all those generals and emperors so that, in glory and triumph, they could become the momentary masters of a fraction of a dot. Think of the endless cruelties visited by the inhabitants of one corner of this pixel on the scarcely distinguishable inhabitants of some other corner, how frequent their misunderstandings, how eager they are to kill one another, how fervent their hatreds.*

> *Our posturings, our imagined self-importance, the delusion that we have some privileged position in the Universe, are challenged by this point of pale light. Our planet is a lonely speck in the great enveloping cosmic dark. In our obscurity, in all this*

vastness, there is no hint that help will come from elsewhere to save us from ourselves.

The Earth is the only world known so far to harbor life. There is nowhere else, at least in the near future, to which our species could migrate. Visit, yes. Settle, not yet. Like it or not, for the moment the Earth is where we make our stand.

It has been said that astronomy is a humbling and charac-ter-building experience. There is perhaps no better demonstration of the folly of human conceits than this distant image of our tiny world. To me, it underscores our responsibility to deal more kindly with one another, and to preserve and cherish the pale blue dot, the only home we've ever known.[3]

Twenty five hundred years before Carl Sagan saw our Earth suspended in space, the author of Psalm 8, perhaps feeling small and anxious, declared:

O Lord, our Sovereign, how majestic is your name in all the earth! You have set your glory above the heavens.

Out of the mouths of babes and infants you have founded a bulwark because of your foes, to silence the enemy and the avenger.

When I look at your heavens, the work of your fingers, the moon and the stars that you have established;

what are human beings that you are mindful of them, mor-tals that you care for them?

Overwhelmed by the vastness of his three-story universe, the Psalmist looks to the micro and discovers something just as breath-taking as the universe's immensity:

Yet you have made them a little lower than God, and crowned them with glory and honor.

---

3   https://www.goodreads.com/work/quotes/1816628-pale-blue-dot-a-vision-of-the-human-future-in-space

Piglet's Process   13

*You have given them dominion over the works of your hands;
you have put all things under their feet, all sheep and oxen, and
also the beasts of the field,*

*the birds of the air, and the fish of the sea, whatever passes
along the paths of the seas.*

*O Lord, our Sovereign, how majestic is your name in all
the earth!*

Residents of a Small, and these days, Anxious Planet, we are
yet at the heart of God's own adventure. Humble humanity is not
lost in the cosmos, but has a calling, a vocation, to experience its
own holiness and claim our role as caretakers and nurturers of this
good Earth. Though we have shirked our responsibility, thinking
we are the center of the universe and that life exists solely for our
gratification, we can rediscover the wonder of garden, woodland,
and sea, and reclaim our place as God's companions in preserving
and protecting the small blue dot upon which live.

Theological Adventurers. Piglet may not know it, but he is a
theological and spiritual adventurer. Theological reflection has no
minimum age or educational requirements. The simple may be
just as erudite as well the well-educated, and often just as insight-
ful. Listen to your children and grandchildren or the youngsters
at church or in your neighborhood and you will hear the voices of
theologians and spiritual guides. The Tao, the mind of Christ, is
still fresh in them. There is no guile, simply trust in the wonder
of this present moment. The most profound theological reflection
is often the simplest and most straightforward. Think of Jesus'
affirmations: "You are the light of the world," "I have come that
you might have abundant life," "I am the vine and you are the
branches." Words any child can understand, and images that will
transform your world.

One of the greatest theologians of the twentieth century, Karl
Barth was once asked to summarize his whole theology — encom-
passing thousands of pages and scores of books — in one sentence.

The Swiss theologian responded to his inquisitor: "Yes, I can. In the words of a song I learned at my mother's knee: 'Jesus loves me, this I know, for the Bible tells me so.'" Can God's relationship with us be summarized by a children's song? "Sing ho!" as Winnie the Pooh chants. "You better believe it." Just remember that brief phrase from John's Gospel — for God so loved the world. Just remember that you have to be a child to experience God's realm. Celebrate Jesus' shushing adults, who were complaining about children interrupting his message, and placing those rowdy and boisterous children in his arms and blessing them.

Theology begins with wonder and adventure, with the vision of an enchanted reality of resurrections and burning bushes, and inspires amazement at the sheer fact that we woke up this morning, and now that we are awake, "What's next? What surprises will come our way?"

What adventures have you had today? Where were you surprised or astounded? When did you experience awe and wonder? Or, did you go about business as usual, spirits tamped down by the morning news and your agenda for the day. Yet, in the 100 Aker Wood and in the world of poets, prophets, and theologians, nothing is ordinary. The magi follow a star and the shepherds hear a choir of angels. God's Child is born in a cave to simple working-class parents. Any moment can invite you to be part of a holy adventure with angels, stars, stuffed bears, and magi as your companions.

This morning, I woke up to the crispness of wind and a sky full of stars. Like the author of Psalm 19, my heart is filled with joy as I, too, affirm that "the heavens declare the glory of God."

An early Greek philosopher is reputed to have said, "Every day brings a new god." Every day is full of promise and possibility. The holiness of each day calls us to praise and prayerfulness, even if we never enter a mosque, ashram, temple, or sanctuary. Each morning, as I take my first footsteps on Craigville Beach, hugging Nantucket Sound, I embrace the novelty of creation as I chant, "This is the day that God has made; I will rejoice and be glad in it." (adapted from Psalm 118:24) Echoing that same sentiment, another biblical writer affirmed:

> *God's steadfast love of the Lord never ceases, God's mercies never come to an end; they are new every morning; great is your faithfulness.* (Lamentations 3:22-23)

Today, you are invited on an adventure. There is no way of avoiding the novelty of this moment, regardless of how jaded you may be. Today was created by Love. Today was inspired by Beauty. Despite the bloviations of politicians and the greed of corporations, there is an Underlying Wisdom that bursts forth when you least expect it. Gentle Providence guides your steps and missteps. Mercy and Love bless us each morning as the gifts of God's wise but mostly hidden creativity. Who knows — along the way you might be joined by a lyrical bear and an attentive little pig?

Piglet and Process. Theology is, as philosopher Alfred North Whitehead asserts, an adventure of ideas. But, what can a fictional creature, and a Small Animal at that, teach us about theology — about our visions of God's relationship to the world and humankind, and the realities of creativity, freedom, forgiveness, inspiration, and death? What can a child's "imaginary" playmate tell us about healing and salvation? How can that Small Animal Piglet help us understand the wisdom of theological vision known as process theology that many adults find incomprehensible?

It may be a stretch, but I believe that the glory of God is manifest as fully in a stuffed toy as the perorations of a televangelist or the ruminations of an armchair theologian. If the whole universe shapes each moment of experience, as the philosopher Alfred North Whitehead speculates, then the minutest particle in outer space or a stuffed pig awakening in the 100 Aker Wood can also declare the wisdom and creativity of God.

Piglet might have trouble understanding theology as it's taught in seminaries and graduate schools. Still, he would respect higher education, just as he respects Christopher Robin's elementary school studies. He would enjoy hearing the words theologians use just as he enjoys hearing Owl using big words to describe life in the 100 Aker Wood. He might even be so enraptured that he would go into a trance, and almost fall off one of the limbs of his tree house, just he almost did during one of Owl's discourses. To Piglet, theology and philosophy, the quest to understand the holiness of life and the wonder of each day, is ultimately about lived experience, about navigating spiritually and ethically in the day to day life of the 100 Aker Wood and interacting with all the unique and quirky characters living in the Wood.

Living theology is pastoral and practical, for Piglet, and process theology is no exception. Living process theology helps us to be brave when we want to run away. It inspires generosity when we want to hold on tight to what we have. It lures us on adventures and takes us on uncharted pathways when we want to cling to the familiar. Process theology comes alive in everyday encounters and helps us see holiness in the complaints of curmudgeonly Eeyore and the meanderings of a Silly Old Bear named Winnie the Pooh.

While Piglet would be perplexed by most philosophical jargon, I think if it were explained to him in the language of the 100 Aker Wood, he would see that process theology provides a vision of reality that can illumine his daily adventures with friends, as well as enlighten students in a seminary classroom, congregants hearing a preacher's message, believers on a quest for understanding, and seekers meandering in search of faith to live by.

TWELVE PRINCIPLES
OF THE PROCESS WAY

When I told him about the twelve principles of process the-
ology, Piglet asked: "Why twelve? Is that a special number?" "I'm
not sure," I responded. Maybe it's because of the twelve days of
Christmas, twelve disciples, twelve months of the year, or just be-
cause I couldn't think of any more." "Twelve's a good number,"
Piglet averred. "But, it could be five or fifteen, right, professor?"

"Yes, Piglet, process theology has no dogmas and is always
open to revision. Maybe, there's only five, but just for today, let's
do twelve, even if I seem to repeat myself," I replied.

"Then twelve it is, but it could be ten tomorrow?" Piglet
concluded. "Or thirteen," he continued, not content with his
conclusion.

Process theology has existed as long as humans have experienced the interplay of stability and change and considered the
relationship between the predictability of the passing seasons and
the unique and fleeting reality of each new day. Hebraic wisdom
givers proclaimed that all flesh is grace, but also that God is ev-
er-faithful. Greek philosophers affirmed that everything flows and
that you can't step in the same rivers twice, and yet they believed
that there is a reality whose changeless beauty inspires every human achievement. Piglet knows that each day is filled with new
adventures, and yet he's also proud of having a sign announcing
"Trespassers W" as a tribute to his grandfather and the traditions
of his family.

For process thinkers, the process itself is the reality. In this
precious and unique moment, arising and perishing, we discover

our vocation as artists and creators, as companions with a Greater Creativity that shapes our days. In this moment of creative transformation, tradition and novelty, and past and present, give birth to new creation and constant adventure. Rejoice in the moment, for soon it will pass. Open to your heart to the wondrous and unrepeatable flow of life.

When we think of the emergence of process theology in our time, names like Alfred North Whitehead, Henri Bergson, and Charles Hartshorne initially come to mind. These philosophers saw life as an ever-flowing stream. We might also recall the impact of more contemporary theologians such as John Cobb, Bernard Loomer, Henry Nelson Wieman, Schubert Ogden, and the their students and theological heirs, David Griffin, Bob Mesle, Marjorie Suchocki, Catherine Keller, Jay McDaniel, Patricia Adams Farmer, Ron Farmer, Donna Bowman, Tripp Fuller, Philip Clayton, Rita Nakashima Brock, Rebecca Parker, Tom Oord, and a whole new generation of process theologians emerging today.

To this list, Piglet averred "They might even think of you, Bruce, though they would have to look hard to find you walking on a Cape Cod beach."

Process thinkers, professional or lay, gaze in amazement at the passage of time, the evolution of the universe, and our own brief but wonderful adventures in our time and place, giving thanks for yesterday and saying "yes" to tomorrow.

Yes, the process is the reality. Yet, the process is not aimless, but — like Pooh and Piglet — is guided by a vision, a way of looking at the world that is fresh and exciting and joins us all in a vast, intricate, and dynamic web of life. No one knows where the path will lead, but a Gentle Providence walks beside us guiding our steps and inspiring us to forge new pathways.

Piglet doesn't like long explanations, but he understands affirmations. So here are twelve affirmations or principles, characterizing process theology.

I've checked them out with Piglet, and his response was, "If you speak slowly, I'll understand, and then I'll explain to Pooh

*Bear, but then again, by the time I finish the first affirmation,
he'll assert that it's time for a honey break!"*

1) Life is Change. We live in a dynamic, lively, ever-changing
universe. Like the waves breaking on Cape Cod beaches, the wind
blowing through your hair, and a baby's development in her mother's womb, living things are in constant motion. Life never stands
still but is a creative advance into the future. The seasons change
in the 100 Aker Wood and newcomers like Kanga and Roo turn
everything upside down. In an ever-changing world, faithfulness
to what's best in life and fidelity to the Holy, means growth and
though Piglet doesn't know much about God, he thinks God is the
primary agent of change. God is the "most moved mover," living
in dynamic relationship with all creation, as one process theologian
asserted.

2) We're All Connected. "Ubuntu," chants South African artists and theologians. "I am because of you and we are all in this
together." Life is a web of relationships in which the well-being
of one depends on the well-being of all and the well-being of the
totality depends on the flourishing of the many parts. No person,
community, or nation is an island. While we all need solitude to
grow spiritually, as the philosopher Whitehead notes, we are also
immersed in the stream of life. The whole universe — even the stars
in another galaxy- shape each moment of our lives.

3) Experience Everywhere. We live in an enchanted universe
in which all things emerge from their experiences of the world.
The heavens shout out God's praise and so do butterflies, babies,
a child's imagination, and a stuffed pig and his friends. To exist is
to be in relationship, and to exist is also to be a center of experience. Rocks don't think or have selves like humans but they are
composed of lively momentary occasions of experience, connected
with one another. The trees of the Wood are alive and whisper to
one another, sharing wisdom to all who listen.

4) Creativity Everywhere. To be is to experience and to experience is to create. You are an artist, but so is every creature,
according to its complexity of experience. Each moment of ex-

perience is an artistic achievement, synthesizing the intricacy of the environment in its own process of self-creation. Creativity is universal, even at the cellular level, as our T-cells recognize and respond to "invaders" to protect the body and our heart rate and circulation change moment by moment to reflect our moods. Some scientists assert that water crystals and plants respond to the order and chaos of their environments. When you speak words of love to the plants in your kitchen herb garden, their rejoicing leads to flourishing. Anger produces crystalline chaos. Treasure the past but remember that we honor the past best by our creativity in this present moment.

5) Value Where You Least Expect It. To exist and to create is to be valuable, whether or not it benefits anyone else. While a degree of destruction is essential to survival and evolution, just as wood must burn to produce a warm winter blaze in your fireplace or around a camp fire, reverence for life is necessary to preserve the holiness of each moment's experience, whether human, non-human, or plant. Whatever exists matters and deserves our gratitude and respect. As Pooh would tell you, enjoy the honey and care for the hive!

6) Small is Beautiful and Matters, Too. Piglet is a Very Small Animal and yet his little life brings beauty to the 100 Aker Wood. A butterfly flapping its wings in Pacific Grove may alter the weather patterns on Cape Cod. In the lively, interdependence of life, each moment can change the world. Everything matters in bringing joy or pain to the world, in awakening new possibilities or closing the door to the future. Small as you may think you are, you can be a hero, saving the day like Piglet, when Pooh and Owl are trapped in a fallen tree house.

7) Adventure Around Every Corner. Each moment is an adventure. "God's mercies are new every morning." You can find the North Pole, where you least expect it, and a Woozle is waiting to surprise you. Each day brings the hope of excitement. Boredom is a metaphysical impossibility for those who recognize they are always on Holy Ground.

8) *We Walk in Beauty.* The world is the paint brush of divinity. The philosopher Whitehead speculates that the aim of the universe is toward the production of beauty, and beauty emerges from that right blend of order and novelty, uniformity and contrast, tradition and innovation. The clouds scudding over the 100 Aker Wood are beautiful and so is a tattered Teddy Bear that accompanies a child to bed. The Divine Artist lovingly and generously inspires beauty throughout the universe.

9) *Fat Soul Spirituality.* My theological friend Patricia Adams Farmer talks about the virtue of having a "fat soul."

> *When he heard this phrase, Piglet asked if she was talking about Winnie the Pooh and then looking over at me, he quipped, "You've got a fat soul. I can tell because you've got a soft belly!"*

> *A bit embarrassed, I replied, "You're right, but it's not so much the size of your waistline as how big your world is. We're meant to reach out to the world, to embrace novelty, to welcome strangers, and to delight in diversity."*

Fat souls have "size," as the process theologian Bernie Loomer affirmed, and having a big soul joins you to the whole universe and that little child who's holding your hand. Growth involves balancing past and future and familiar and strange.

10) *Soul Friends.* Spiritual friendships, *anamcara*, are at the heart of reality. Spiritual friendships deepen our relationship with God and the creation.

> *"A theology of soul friends, now that's interesting," Piglet ruminated.*

> *"Do theologians care about Pooh and me walking hand in hand, and going on unexpected adventures?"*

> *"Yes," I responded, "We create each other by our love, and sometimes there are special people who show you what God's like and help you discover your own divinity — that holiness that's the heart of your life."*

Process theologians believe that without love, there can't be theology. God loves the world and we find God when we love each other, especially those people whose love opens our heart to the Holy. A friend of the soul, what the Celts called *anamcara,* is the mirror of God, revealing to us our own divinity and vocation.

> *"Well, that's Pooh and me," Piglet chirped.*

11) Earthly Good. Everything we do matters, and every action shapes the universe. What happens in our lives brings beauty or ugliness to life. Our lives may be brief, but they make a difference. Even if we live on into eternity, this "now" is the only moment there is. This earth is our responsibility and we are artists of beauty whose love protects polar bears and arctic ice bergs, butterflies and milk weed plants, hungry children and weary elders. Everything we do lasts forever, and like a pebble thrown in a pond, radiates across the universe.

> *"What happens in the Wood really matters. Stories once told to a child, they're still alive, bring joy to other children, like your son and grandchildren," Piglet averred. "I really like it that even an Anxious Animal's story can change the world."*

> *"Yes, Piglet," I responded, "You are part of that wondrous and intricate ripple, living forever in God and in the experiences of children and adults everywhere."*

12) Providence Gently Moves. God's Gentle Providence gives life to all creation and guides our steps providing possibilities and inspiring ideas. God's power is revealed in our freedom and creativity. God does not control but invites and inspires.

> *When he saw I was writing about God, Piglet admitted, "I don't know much about God. It's a word you don't hear very often in the 100 Aker Wood. But I do know about surprises, unexpected encounters, friends who rescue me when flood waters are rising. I do know about the Enchanted Wood and Christopher Robin's imagination. Maybe, I don't need the big words, because God is the air we breathe and the wind that blows."*

I countered, "I think that's God, don't you?"

Piglet responded, "Yes, God is with us, right here, whether or not we notice it. God is like the breeze, blowing through the Woods and waking me up to adventure. God is what gives me the courage to search for Woozles or go on an Expotition. Maybe, God is the spirit that inspires our Expotition."

Whether in the 100 Aker Wood or our own lives, there is a Gentle Providence that nudges us forward on the path, sometimes through a synchronous encounter, a wise intuition, a dream that unravels a mystery, an inspiring thought, or a heart-felt identification with the suffering of other persons. God seldom announces God's presence, but quietly and persistently, and sometimes dramatically, we feel a force for good, find ourselves part of a larger movement toward justice and beauty, or embrace of a new possibility. That Gentle Providence is God with us and God in us.

The twelve principles of process theology are really about relationships and faithfulness through all the seasons of life. These days, while the Wood is in danger, and we must by our simple actions join God in healing the world. We need to remember that we are the change we are looking for, whether in the Wood or our own neighborhoods. The residents of the 100 Aker Wood are always on the move — holding hands, sharing stories, looking for adventure. Sometimes they go their separate ways, following their own passions. But, at the end of the day, they're all together, tucked in bed beside Christopher Robin or sitting around a festive table celebrating Eeyore's birthday or Piglet's bravery. They are one despite their individual uniqueness. We are born for each other, live for each other, and find our way home with each other. Love never ends. If there's a heaven to imagine, it's in the walking and loving, and seeing each other only with the eyes of love.

"Twelve principles?" Piglet asked. "I quit counting after five. I think there could be just three or fifteen, or maybe even more. But this process theology you're telling me about sounds like my

life — adventures with friends, who rejoice in the beauty of each day and the wonder of each other."

And in response, I said, "Amen."

CHAPTER ONE

LIFE IS CHANGE

"I say, I wonder what's going to happen exciting today?" said Piglet.[4]

The process is the reality, so says philosopher Alfred North Whitehead.

> *"I think I get that," Piglet notes. "Today is a new day, and every day when I wake up, I wonder what exciting thing will happen. There are lot of things about the Woods that stay the same, but each day, leaves fall, the stream flows, the wind blows, and the clouds roll by. Just this morning Pooh and I lay on our backs watching the clouds scud by and tried to imagine the clouds as creatures sailing above us. The shapes in the clouds changed moment by moment. I saw elephants and clowns and sharks and whales. Pooh, saw honey pots of every size and shape. I even spied a Heffalump, but then it became a Woozle, and I was glad they were faraway. Yesterday, it was sunny and warm, but today the rain is falling, I'm a little worried that the creek will flood and I'll be surrounded by water and won't be able to leave my house."*

Whitehead once noted that the primary metaphysical realities — that is, the ways things are at their depths, can be described by a hymn:

> *Abide with me*

> *Fast falls the eventide.*

As I write these words, the days are growing shorter as we move toward Winter Solstice. It's four o'clock and the sun is setting as I

---

4   A.A. Milne, *The World of Winnie the Pooh* (New York: Penguin Books, 1985), 168.

pick up my grandchildren at school. Fast falls the eventide. Soon
the stars will be out and a full moon will rise on the horizon. But,
before you know it, I'll be waking up to a new day, sunrise on the
beach, clear and cold, walking along like Piglet, saying my morning
prayers and delighting in the movement of the waves in Nantucket Sound. Life is changing moment by moment, but something
abides There's a pattern to the changes makes life dependable and
helps us find our way through each day's adventures.

In life, change and constancy, novelty and familiarity, and innovation and tradition, characterize the experiences and histories of
persons and institutions. In the world of process theology, change
and process are the most important realities. Life is, as Whitehead
noted, a process of perpetual perishing. This very moment arises in
its freshness from a myriad of conscious and unconscious influences
— my desire to write a few words before I pick up my grandchildren, the warmth of the fire in my living room, the comfortable
feeling after having a good lunch, a good strong cup of coffee,
the joy of playing with a puppy, the challenge of responding to a
congregant's questions. In the uniqueness of this moment, all these
factors and many of which I am unaware are brought together in
this holy here and now. But, then before I know it, this sentence is
written. I'm thinking of the next paragraph and some words from
Winnie the Pooh and off we go again. There is never a moment like
this one in all the universe, and yet out of this moment another
unrepeatable moment arises for me, another thought and feeling
tone, a cell in my body morphs into another, or Tigger bounds
through the Wood leaving in his wake glorious chaos.

Philosophers and theologians have struggled to decide which
is most important — change or stability, or process or eternity.
For some, the eternal is the most real. What doesn't change, what's
incorruptible, is what's really important, while the changing and
impermanent flow of life is an illusion, at worst, and the front
porch to eternity at best. Some theologians believe that God never
changes. God knows everything in one unchanging vision. They
believe that change in God or us is from the perfect to the imper-

fect. What we see as history, as the flow of life, has already occurred in the mind of God. God enjoys the perfection of being God, an eternal, unchanging light in which there is neither subtraction nor addition. For God to feel our pain or joy would be subject God to the chance occurrences of earthly life and would tarnish God's heavenly equanimity.

Now, of course, some things don't appear to change. Piglet is proud of the sign posted in front of his home that announces "TRESPASSERS W." Short for "Trespassers William," Piglet's grandfather, the sign reminds Piglet of his heritage, of a long line of Small Animals that bravely navigated the Wood. It gives him courage when he thinks of strange animals he may encounter like Woozles and Heffalumps. But Piglet knows there's more to life than yesterday and that change can be a great gift for us and for God.

> Piglet, who's been looking over my shoulder as I type, interjects, "But wouldn't that be kind of boring, never to change or grow and day after day and have everything the same. An unchanging god doesn't sound very interesting. If God's complete, and doesn't change, then God seems stuck to me — God keeps experiencing things over and over and over again- bad things and good things. It's like hearing Pooh sing one of his songs day after day, and over and over. It's nice the first three or four times, but every day and all the time, even Pooh needs to sing new songs and make up new stories. Wouldn't God get bored? Wouldn't God envy a Small Animal who can do new things and experience new days?"

Once upon a time, the residents of the Wood had to deal with a big change. Kanga and Roo, very strange and hopping animals, had just arrived and disturbed the ecology of the Wood. Rabbit was worried that these intruders would change everything, so he hatched a plan to let them know they weren't wanted. He wanted things to remain the same and feared that any changes would be for the worse. As you may recall, Rabbit's plan involved substituting Piglet for Roo and frightening Kanga into leaving. Alas, the plan failed. Kanga discovered the switch and led Piglet on a merry ride and to a soapy bath, much to Piglet's chagrin.

> *"Don't remind me of that mishap," Piglet averred. "I really got sucked into something stupid. I just wasn't thinking and went along with Rabbit's scheme to preserve order by banishing newcomers from the Wood. Thank goodness the plot failed. Nowadays, Rabbit and Roo are best friends and Kanga mothers us all. Change can be wonderful and difference adds zest and joy to the Wood."*

Lots of people fear change. They are worried about newcomers to their own particular Wood: refugees from other countries, immigrants working in our nation's stores and agricultural industry, or people from other faith traditions. They want to go back to a time when people, especially men, of European extract dominated everything. They don't like the idea of people from other countries — and of course, their parents came from other countries! — shaping the future of our country. But change is inevitable. Our goal, in all life's necessary and inevitable changes, is to remain faithful to our highest values and embrace change as an opportunity for creativity and hospitality.

A church historian Jaraslov Pelikan once stated that "tradition is the living faith of the dead; traditionalism is the dead faith of the living. Tradition lives in conversation with the past, while remembering where we are and when we are and that it is we who have to decide. Traditionalism supposes that nothing should ever be done for the first time, so all that is needed to solve any problem is to arrive at the supposedly unanimous testimony of this homogenized tradition."

> *"I like that," Piglet replied. "I don't know much about theology, but I think God remembers everything, provides enough order for us to find our way, and then sends us on Expotitions and Adventures to make life interesting. I'm proud of Trespassers W and the generations of Small Animals before me, but this is my time to shine, to have adventures, to be frightened and then boldly face my fears in my own way, just as they did in their time."*

"A writer in the Bible said more or less the same thing," I agreed. "The author of the Book of Lamentations 3:22-23 proclaimed:

The steadfast love of the LORD *never ceases, his mercies never come to an end; they are new every morning; great is your faithfulness."*

That could be Piglet's motto. God's love never ends, but the shape of God's love is never the same from one day to the next. Faithfulness is not about changeless perfection but constancy of vision and ethics in a world of change. God is constantly doing a new thing, flowing through all things, presenting new possibilities and then moving on to the next thing. To the chagrin of those who prefer eternity to time, God is the agent of restlessness and adventure. God delights in creative transformation and novelty. As another scripture proclaims, "Behold, I do a new thing." (Isaiah 43:19) In speaking of God's Spirit, Jesus once said, "the wind blows where it chooses and you hear the sound of it, but you do not know where it comes from or where it goes." (John 3:8)

Piglet nodded his head emphatically. "I sure know about the wind. I was in Owl's tree house when the wind blew it down. The wind is alive and always moving. It can't stand still. You mean that's how God is?" "Yes, Piglet," I responded. "Life is process for God, too. God is the breath that blows the clouds, the energy that radiates from the son, the joy of the athlete, and the vision that inspires tomorrow."

Some biblical scholars have noted that the God of scripture is a living, changing, challenging God. Faithful in God's promises, God is constantly inspiring the people to look toward new horizons. Life is here in the moment and in the moment to come. The world was created "good" and not "perfect" or complete, for the complete can never grow or change, and God is the agent in the quest for beauty, justice, and Shalom. The changing God is embedded in the messiness of life, whether it is a stable in Bethlehem, liberating the oppressed, healing the sick, or challenging bloodthirsty rulers. Changing, growing, living, and dying, Jesus brings life and light to all things. "Love God in the world of the flesh," as W.H. Auden counsels, and the universe will burst forth in wonder and beauty, and you will discover that God is changing beside you.

CHAPTER TWO

WE'RE ALL
CONNECTED

*"What did it look like?" [asked Christopher Robin]. "Like it
had the biggest head you ever saw, Christopher Robin. A great
enormous thing like — like nothing. A huge big — well, like
a — I don't know — like an enormous big nothing. Like a jar."
[Piglet responded]*

*"Well," said Christopher Robin, putting on his shoes. "I shall
go and look at it. Come on."*

*Piglet wasn't afraid if he had Christopher Robin with him,
so off they went...* [5]

Piglet is a little uncomfortable of fancy theological language.
When Owl shares his wisdom, Piglet can't help but admire his
erudite friend, but then he asks himself: "What on earth was he
talking about. It sounded intelligent, but I can't make any sense of
anything he said." Although Piglet has a good sized brain — much
larger than Winnie the Pooh's, according to Christopher Robin —
he is more comfortable with plain-spoken theology, theology that
you can touch like Pooh Bear's hands and taste like haycorns and
honey. Like Etty Hillsum, he would prefer to be a "thinking heart"
to being an "erudite thinker."

Piglet wants his words to reflect his whole self — body, mind,
spirit, and emotions — as revealed in his meanderings with friends
in the 100 Aker Wood. Piglet is a practical theologian — his theology is worked out in experience: in walks in the Wood, in fleeing
from angry honey bees, in holding hands with Pooh, and finding
courage when he wants to hide.

5   Ibid., 72.

I shared a quote from Bishop Desmond Tutu of South Africa with Piglet one afternoon as we watched the clouds scudding by in the Wood behind my home, two friends sharing the joy of being together:

Bringing people together is what I call "ubuntu," which means "I am because we are. Far too often people think of themselves as just individuals, separated from one another, whereas you are connected and what you do affects the whole world. When you do well, it spreads out, it is for the whole of humanity."

Piglet nodded his head and responded, "I get that. Ubuntu is Pooh singing a song about me and the two of us searching for a Woozle or going on Expotition to the North Pole. The adventure is exciting but what makes it special is a hand to hold when I hear a strange sound and begin to feel anxious. Ubuntu is remembering my grandfather Trespassers W and giving thanks for my family tree. Ubuntu is giving Eeyore a balloon, even it's already popped, and holding hands with Christopher Robin and moving in with Pooh Bear when I give up my home so Owl can have a place to stay." And, I replied, "Ubuntu is the two of us talking and your stories helping me write a book for Piglets and people just like you. You are a part of me, and without you and your friends, I'd be reading pulp fiction or watching the news this morning! Ubuntu is knowing my friend, Wendy, who introduced Pooh stories to me nearly fifty years ago is still in my heart, though she has passed away. Ubuntu is praying for my little grandsons, my son, and my wife Kate, and knowing wherever we are, we are connected. Without them, I would not be me."

One of my teachers Bernard Loomer initially coined the term "process-relational" theology. The process is the reality, that's obvious Loomer thought. But, the process is intricately connected at every level. Life is change and the change is the result of the interplay of our creativity and the world around us. Change is always relational. The philosopher Whitehead once asserted that the whole universe conspires to create each moment of experience. Every experience we have emerges from our relationship to the environment, near and far, and past and present. What happens in Moscow or on America's borderlands today shapes my life at a deep level, just as the placement of the stars and planets on the day of my birth provided the energy that — to some degree — shapes the rest of my life. The child is the father to the adult. Mature adults grow from small children and childhood experiences shape adult values.

We live in an intricately interdependent world of relationships. The air we breathe, the water we drink, the touch of loved ones, the feeling tones and values of culture, all shape who we are from moment to moment. As I write these words, there's a lot of anxiety about the direction our nation is taking. Many of us believe that we have turned our back on ethical values, condoned injustice toward immigrants and persons from the Middle East, and have purposely chosen environmentally-destructive policies. What happens in the United States will determine whether or not the Wood will flourish in the years ahead. Will enterprising entrepreneurs see the Wood as a perfect place for a resort or mine it for minerals? Will the gradually rising temperatures lead to disastrous changes in the weather, including last year's flood that left Piglet stranded in his treehouse? Will little animals survive opening up wilderness lands and dumping coal waste in steams? Will Cape Cod where I live be a victim of global climate change and our headlong race to mine and drill the oceans?

Today, people talk a lot about ecology and climate change and as you can see that's a big issue in the Wood. Close to nature, the creatures of the 100 Aker Wood are attuned to every nuance in the weather patterns. They don't always have words to describe "God," but they revel in "beauty" and know, with the philosopher Whitehead, that the goal of the universe, revealed in cloud, stream, and tree as well as their own experiences, is toward creating more and more beauty. What humans do has an impact on polar ice caps, plankton, rivers, streams, lakes, and oceans. Coal power plants destroy the atmosphere and raise ocean temperatures. People in Beijing wear face masks because of air pollution and here on Cape Cod we worry about the potential harm caused by an out-of-date nuclear power plant less than thirty miles away from my home. In an interdependent universe, there is nowhere to run and nowhere to hide, and there is also no place where we are isolated from the loving thoughts and creative actions of our companions on planet Earth.

The English poet Francis Thompson affirmed that "Thou canst not still a flower without troubling a star." We are through and through relational. Who we are and what we do truly matters, and what's going on in the lives of others matters to us, shapes us as persons and denizens of the Wood, even when we are unaware of its long-term impact.

The Grace of Interdependence meditated through sun, rain, flora, fauna, and relationships gives us life and breath. The Grace of Interdependence is simply "God with us and in us" or as some process theologians say, "God in all things and all things in God," not making a fuss about God's handiwork, but delighting in the constant creativity in which we live and move and have our being. If God is anything in the world, God is the inspiration to creativity and the counterforce to needless and unnecessary destruction. God is not aloof, or stuck in some timeless eternity, immune from the joy and pain of the world, God is in the midst of the wondrous messiness of life, the one to whom all hearts are open and all desires known.

> *"You mean God is here, and not on some faraway planet or sitting on a throne high up on a cloud?" Piglet asked.*

> *"Yes, Piglet, that's what I think. God touches us with love every moment and we touch God by what we do each day. Sometimes God's heart must be broken by our destructive behaviors, but I am sure God rejoices when Kanga and Roo are welcomed to the Wood or when we discover that a Small Animal can be a hero. God delights in the color purple, sunrise on Cape Cod, lovers embracing, and people of other religions sharing in a common purpose. It may really upset God, as author Alice Walker says, when we walk by a purple flower and don't pause to be amazed.*

God may mourn when we destroy a forest or pollute a stream to
make the quick profit or political point."

Everything we do, process theologians affirm, is our gift to
God, and our contribution to God's experience of the world.
When we love others, we truly love God, who rejoices in the love
that Pooh and Piglet have for each other and Christopher Robin
and Pooh making a pact to remember each other. The ultimate
horizon for ethics is our response to the questions: "Will we give
God a more beautiful or ugly world by our actions? Will we enable
God to be more present in our world by opening our hearts to 'the
least of these' or will we close the door to divine possibilities by
turning away from God's vision of Shalom, of justice and beauty?"

For process theologians, prayer is the ultimate act of Graceful
Interdependence. Prayer connects us with people across the globe
and joins past, present, and future in a vision of health and whole-
ness. When we pray, we connect with creation both near and far.
In the words of some scientists and physicians, prayer is the prime
example of "non-local causation" or "distant intentionality." But
however we describe it, our prayers join us with loved ones everywhere and unite us in loving care with people we'll never meet.
Prayer creates a field of loving energy around those for whom we
pray and, I believe, enables God, who is immersed in all our lives,
to be more creative and effective in changing the world for the best.

"That's really interesting," Piglet pondered. "I don't go to
church often, except when Christopher Robin tucks me and Pooh
in his satchel and takes us along for morning prayer at the vil-
lage church. But I think I know what prayer is. Prayer is me
thinking of Pooh, when I go to bed at night, and hoping he gets a
good night's sleep. Prayer is me imagining what adventures we'll
have tomorrow or taking a deep breath and saying 'thanks' when
I wake up in the morning. Prayer is wishing Eeyore could just
for once be happy or worrying with love about Rabbit lost in the
woods. Prayer is knowing that even if I fall in a hole, I can call
out for help, and that someone will find me. Prayer is that extra

ounce of courage that helps me escape Owl's fallen tree to get help
for Pooh and Owl."

"Yes, Piglet, prayer is about connection, relationship, love,
and hope. It's about imagining a better life for us and others and
then doing all we can to make it happen."

"Well, Prof," Piglet speculated, "the whole universe may be
one great prayer. Me thinking of you and you thinking of me,
and everything deep down being the best it can, even when they're
misbehaving."

"Yes, Piglet, that could be it," I replied, "As a follower of
Jesus, named Paul, asserted, "We don't always know what to pray
for, but God's Spirit prays within us in sighs too deep for words."

In process-relational thought, there is no "other." We are all
connected in that dynamic fabric of relatedness, that intricate web
of life, in which — as Martin Luther King asserted — you can't be
what you are meant to be until I am what I am meant to be, and
I can't be what I'm meant to be until you are what you are meant
to be. So, let's root for each other — that we have joy and peace,
and learn great things together as one.

CHAPTER THREE

EXPERIENCE
EVERYWHERE

*[Pooh and Christopher Robin] walked on, thinking of This
and That, and by-and-by they came to an enchanted place on
the very top of the Forest called Galleons Lap, which is sixty-some-
thing trees in a circle; and Christopher Robin knew that it was
enchanted place because nobody had been able to count whether
it was sixty-three or sixty-four, not even when he tied a piece of
string around each tree after he had counted it.* [6]

A wise spiritual teacher once said that if our senses opened and
cleansed, we would see everything as it is and then discover that
everything is infinite. To the residents of the 100 Aker Wood and
the children who read the Winnie the Pooh stories, this statement
is obvious. We live in an enchanted universe, in which stuffed toys
can go on adventures and on blustery days, you can hear the wind
whisper your name. Nothing is quite what it seems. Beneath the
surface, life abounds. A gnarled tree is buzzing with life — and bees
too! A stream sings melodious hymns. Craggy rocks point toward
the heavens and inspire mystics. All things, as the Christian mystic
Meister Eckhardt proclaimed, are words of God, revealing divine
wisdom and creativity and humming their own unique melody.
Moreover, if God is present everywhere, then even the humblest
particle in faraway empty space is a revelation of divinity.

Process theologians believe that we live in an enchanted universe. Deep down, we can find life and experience in everything
that exists. Nothing is completely dead. Nothing is purely objec-
tive and inert. The process is the reality and the reality is made up

---

6   Ibid., 355.

of tiny drops of experience, each varying in its degree of creativity and responsiveness to the world around it.

"What's so special about that?" Piglet asked. "I thought everyone knew that the world is alive. After all, if stuffed animals can go on adventures, who can deny that monkeys, dolphins, and sharks also have a life of their own. Do you mean that some people go through life thinking only humans can think or feel? Every child knows that!"

"Well, Piglet, I believe that all things can feel, even creatures very different from us. Still some people only value human beings or persons who look like themselves. One philosopher, Rene Descartes, separated the world into minds and bodies. He believed that only humans have minds, and only humans can feel joy and pain. Bodies were purely material and without feeling. He thought that non-human animals felt nothing and only appeared to feel pain as a matter of stimulation and response."

"Boy, that's silly, Prof," Piglet replied. "Your little puppy, Tucker, just two months old, really wanted your attention this morning. He wanted to be petted, fed, and played with. He couldn't understand why you needed to pick up your computer while he was there ready to play. He jumped and whined. That's a sign that he knows what's going on and that he has wants and needs, and likes to be touched and held, just like you do."

"I know, but these philosophers thought that was just automatic. And if animals don't really feel anything, then you can treat them anyway you want — you could put them in factory farms or traumatize them just to make the right cologne. And, of course, some people would rather make money than preserve an endangered species. Nothing is sacred to them, it seems, except how much money they can make. Just look at the rain forests and the polar ice caps. Animals don't feel and the only green that matters is a dollar bill!"

"Tell that to a purring cat or a barking dog, or frankly to a stuffed toy, we know better than that," Piglet objected.

"You know, Piglet, just today over pecan pie and coffee with a few friends, I heard an account of a vineyard owner who plays classical music to provide spiritual nourishment for his grape vines. I looked it up on the internet, and while the science isn't conclusive yet, the plants seem to enjoy the music. According to the vintner, the plants seemed to mature faster under the influence of gentle sounds. Mozart, Haydn, Vivaldi and Mahler were staples on the initial playlist running 24 hours a day."[7]

Process theologians and philosophers use the word "panexperientialism" to describe the universality of experience. In other words, "experience is everywhere." Now to someone who hasn't been to the 100 Aker Wood the notion of an enchanted and experiential universe is ridiculous. "Rocks and tables don't experience anything," they object. "This chair isn't alive. It's inert and unmoving." But, what about the reports that describe grapes flourishing when they hear music, water crystals responding to their emotional environment, and studies suggesting that plants respond positively to affirmations and words of love?

Process thinkers agree that a rock as a whole doesn't have a mind or a central nervous system and that tables don't have emotions. But they are thinking of something much more subtle. While rocks, chairs, tables, grape vines and laptops don't feel the world the way we do and they don't have a central personality that organizes the world and imagines new possibilities or deep emotions like love, fear, delight, and anxiety, within these apparently "dead" objects, you will find a universe of experience. Tiny droplets of experience — actual occasions, atoms, whatever you want to call them — that are buzzing about, touching one another and shaping one another, living and dying, beneath the calm exterior. Just look through an

---

7   http://archive.wired.com/science/discoveries/news/2007/06/music_and_wine

electron microscope at a piece of wood or the cells in your body and you'll see how alive the universe is.

Mystics have always known that the world was alive and that a Living God fashions a living world. The last words of the Psalms proclaim, "let everything that breathes praise God." (Psalm 150:6) A few chapters before, the Psalm writer, enchanted by God's creative wisdom reflected in all things, proclaimed:

> *Praise the* LORD! *Praise the* LORD *from the heavens; praise him in the heights!*

> *Praise him, all his angels; praise him, all his host!*

> *Praise him, sun and moon; praise him, all you shining stars!*

> *Praise him, you highest heavens, and you waters above the heavens!*

> *Let them praise the name of the* LORD, *for he commanded and they were created.*

> *He established them forever and ever; he fixed their bounds, which cannot be passed.*

> *Praise the* LORD *from the earth, you sea monsters and all deeps,*

> *fire and hail, snow and frost, stormy wind fulfilling his command!*

> *Mountains and all hills, fruit trees and all cedars!*

> *Wild animals and all cattle, creeping things and flying birds!*

> *Kings of the earth and all peoples, princes and all rulers of the earth!*

Young men and women alike, old and young together!
(Psalm 148:1-12)

You can't praise God, if you can't experience God's presence. While I'm sure the Psalmist knew the difference between snow-flakes, whales, fruit trees, and humans, the singer also knew that the universe was alive and permeated with God's creative wisdom. The heavens declare the glory of God and so do the cells of our bodies. Jesus knew that, too. Grasses, lilies, and sparrows matter to God, because they all share in God's beauty and wisdom. Centuries later, St. Francis of Assisi described a living universe in which sun, moon, stars, flowing waters, and singing birds praise their Creator. Today, philosophers and scientists — and even a few politicians — are catching up with little children and mystics and are rediscovering a universe of experience, a re-enchanted universe in which birdsongs are melodies of joy and humpbacked whales write love songs.

"Sing ho! my friend Pooh chants at the wonder of life." Piglet gleefully chirped. "Pooh knows first-hand that bees can experience and respond, because they notice him trying to get their honey and then chase him away. Remember the time he had to jump in the creek to escape their anger! Of course, they're just protecting their hive, and who can blame them. But they know what's going on. They're alive and active and want to live, just like people. And, that little creature Small, you can barely see him, but he wants to live, and we know that without Small the Wood isn't complete."

"Spot on, Piglet. Sometimes philosophers, politicians, and corporate executives aren't as smart as stuffed toys and bees. But, think what they're missing. Their world is boring, lifeless, just something to be manipulated, and not a symphony of wonder and blessing. Maybe someday they'll wake up and realize that mountains are more important than coal mines and polar bears more valuable than profits."

"You're right, Prof, but they need to wake up soon. Without appreciation and gratitude, you think you can do what you want.

You can treat birds and whales like they don't matter. You can act as if nature doesn't have feelings."

"Piglet, I think you're a process theologian. You know how important honoring experience can be. If it doesn't experience, as you said, we can do what we want, because we're not causing any pain. But what if we live in a world of experience, then we'd have to pay attention and change our ways, and discover ways to ease the pain of the non-human world. We'd have to care. Well, it's time for a break. We'll take that up in our next conversation."

CHAPTER FOUR

VALUE WHERE YOU
LEAST EXPECT IT

Pooh!" [Piglet] cried. "There's something climbing up your back."

"I thought there was," said Pooh.

"It's Small!" cried Piglet.

"Oh, that's who it is, is it?" said Pooh.

"Christopher Robin," I've found Small!" cried Piglet.

"Well done, Piglet," said Christopher Robin.[8]

An enchanted and experiential universe inspires us to look for value and beauty everywhere. If a creature can experience joy or sorrow — or even the impact of its environment at some minimal level — then it deserves ethical consideration. The converse is also true. If we assume an animal, plant, or person can't feel, then we can feel justified in treating them anyway we want. We don't have to consider the impact of our actions on them. We can "drill, baby, drill" regardless of its impact on polar bears, aquifers, or sacred grounds. We can relax automobile emission standards, believing that only God and not humans can shape the natural order.

When industrialists and politicians believe that woods, hillsides, and animals have no ability to the experience the world, they have no reason to feel remorse at their destruction. It's just business after all, profits to executive and shareholders trumps any

---

8   Ibid., 230.

care for the non-human world. The same attitude applies to our relationships with people. We use derogatory names to dehumanize our opponents in politics and war or diminish the value of women, homosexuals, refugees, and strangers. Decades ago, Bishop Desmond Tutu called apartheid, the rule of Afrikaners over native Africans, a Christian heresy because it described certain people as second class, inferior, and without moral status. It pronounced some people as created in "the image of God" and others bereft of God's blessing. Their rights could be denied in order to serve the interests of the powerful minority, because they God had intended them to be subservient!

One of my spiritual mentors Howard Thurman, the African American mystic and spiritual leader, describes what happens to both the "oppressor" and the "oppressed" when their ability to experience joy and pain is denied. One autumn, young Howard worked a for a white store owner, raking leaves. As he raked the leaves in piles, the store owner's four-year-old daughter decided to play a game. Whenever she saw a brightly colored leaf, she scattered the whole pile to show it to Howard. Although she meant no harm, she did this several times until Howard lost his patience and told her to stop. When she continued, he threatened to tell her father. Angered by his threat, the young girl jabbed him with a straight pen. When he cried out, the girl responded, "O Howard, that didn't hurt you. You can't feel."[9]

You can't feel! That is the hallmark of racism, sexism, homophobia, and environmental destruction. The minute you admit that another person or animal has feelings, ethically speaking, you must affirm that the other has values and rights apart from your interests. While we enjoy the beauty of the non-human world, the flora and fauna — brooks, mountains, birds, bees, sharks, and whales — have interests of their own that must be balanced with our own interests. Denying the ability of others to experience pain allows us to wantonly destroy them if it benefits us. But, to our sur-

9   Howard Thurman, *With Heart and Mind (New York: Harcourt Brace and Company, 1979), 12.*

prise, the one who lives by denial also loses the ability to experience beauty and may — as the Hebrew prophet Amos asserts — forfeit their experience of God even though they build great churches and have lively worship services. The salvation of the world is found in extending value and ethical consideration beyond ourselves to other humans and the non-human world.

> *Piglet chirped up, "That's what I like about Christopher Robin. He treats us stuffed animals as if we have feelings. He cares for us in the same way he cares for his playmates at school. He has a vivid imagination and he sees more deeply than most people. His imagination allows him to see what adults don't see — a symphony in a flock of geese, a community in a pile of stuffed animals, and enchantment in a grove of trees."*

> *"Piglet, have you ever heard of Albert Schweitzer. He was a bible scholar who became a physician and then went to Africa to provide health care for the indigenous people. He coined a term — reverence for life — to describe what you're talking about. He believed that non-human as well as human life had value and deserved to be treated as holy. He knew that our survival required us to eat vegetables and animals but he also knew that we needed to treat non-humans with care and respect. Alfred North Whitehead said the same thing. Whitehead asserted that 'life is robbery.' Our survival requires the destruction of certain organisms. But we need a good reason — a moral justification — for killing our fellow creatures."*

> *"Small things can be beautiful. We had trouble seeing Small, but we still knew he was important, and we knew being lost might put him in danger," Piglet added.*

> *"Schweitzer spoke of a community of those who bear the mark of suffering. If you can feel pain — or joy — you deserve our care and consideration."*

Vision and imagination are at the heart of ethical thinking. When we can, as Teilhard de Chardin asserted, imagine the "within" of other persons or the non-human world, ethics requires us to recognize that we are united in a vast community of experience — joy and sorrow, delight and pain. We are ultimately one world, even when we must make difficult decisions to affirm our family or nation's right to flourish.

If God treasures birds and lilies of the field, then we must treasure them as well. If a creature can experience pain, we owe it moral consideration. First Americans and other indigenous peoples saw life and beauty everywhere. They still had to eat, and often they ate meat, but they gave thanks to the creatures they consumed. They affirmed that while some killing was necessary for survival, the lives of deer, buffalo, and wild fowl still mattered to the Great Spirit of Life and should matter to them as well.

Today, our attitude toward the non-human world is a matter of life and death for ourselves and the planet. Many business leaders, politicians, and consumers see nature solely as a commodity for human benefit. They prefer making profits to following the words of the prophets. They are willing to lose their souls to gain temporary political power and profit.

From the perspective of process theology, what happens in the non-human world — and the world of strangers — is profoundly spiritual and ethical. It reflects our understanding of the scope of God's love. Accordingly, global climate change isn't just about us, but about the value of the world beyond us, regardless of whether we benefit economically from them. The mountains and flowing streams, the ponds and tide pools, are beautiful even if we never notice. Even if we don't notice them, God does, and God hears the cries of the vulnerable, the refugee, the homeless, the dolphin and chimpanzee, the dying species, the polar bear mother trying to protect her young as ice bergs melt.

> *"That's why we spent so much time looking for Small," Piglet repeated. "He didn't have a big impact on our lives, he was so small and easy to miss, but he mattered to us simply because he was Small. Small made a difference to the Wood just by being himself.*

Small truly is beautiful, a Small Wonder just like me, and in all his Smallness, he is amazing."

"*Isn't that the truth, Piglet, we can find beauty everywhere. Life and beauty surround us. Wonder abounds in every cell and beauty bursts forth from every soul."*

"*I know," Piglet asserted, "because I have a soul. No one may notice this Small Animal. But, this Small Animal can glorify God, feel brave and anxious, and go on adventures and do something wonderful with his life."*

"*Yes, Piglet, you've got soul! You're more amazing than I imagined. The world would be poorer without you. And, as that children's song says, 'Every little soul must shine, must shine, every little soul must shine, must shine.'"*

CHAPTER FIVE

CREATIVITY
EVERYWHERE

[Piglet] had a clever idea. He would go up very quietly to the Six Pine Trees now, peep very cautiously into the Trap, and see if there was a Heffalump there. And if there was, he would go back to bed, and there wasn't, he wouldn't.

Process theology believes that we are all artists of experience. Each moment of our lives emerges from our immediate past, our local environment, and the larger cosmos, and then awaits our moment by moment decisions. Consciously and unconsciously, we experience our previous moods as well as the impact of our own or others' previous decisions. These are the materials that we shape in our own unique way.

Creativity is profoundly relationally. Neither God nor humans nor stuffed animals create out of nothing; we create out of something and that something determines in large measure the canvas of our lives. The limits provided by past experiences and our environment are the womb of possibility for self-creation. The philosopher Alfred North Whitehead affirms that the whole universe conspires to create each moment of experience. Yet, just as there are varying degrees of experience, some simple repetitions of the past, others dynamic and dramatic, there are countless degrees of creativity. Still, in every moment of experience, both human and non-human, something novel and unrepeatable occurs.

Every moment is a creative synthesis of the past, leaning toward an open and undecided future. Piglet goes exploring in search of a Heffalump. He's a bit apprehensive but he persists in his quest. What he finds in the Trap will shape his response. Either way, whether he goes back to bed or continues searching, he's creating a future by the decisions he makes in the present moment.

The writing of the Winnie the Pooh books was an act of creative transformation and artistry. From the twenty six letters of the English alphabet, an imaginative story burst forth. Perhaps its origins were in A.A. Milne's fantasy life. It grew and blossomed in bedtime stories with his son and then came to fruition in the writing and re-writing of the text. But, even then, the book's journey was unfinished. Readers like my friend Wendy, and later me, shaped the stories imaginatively as we shared them with others. Listeners, like my son and two grandchildren, created their own imaginative pictures of Winnie, Piglet, Eeyore, and the residents of the 100 Aker Wood as they played with stuffed animals in our great room or met the Winnie the Pooh characters over breakfast at Disneyworld. Writers like Benjamin Hoff, author of the *Tao of Pooh,* and me explored the connection between a cuddly, rotund bear and ancient wisdom. Screenwriters and artists visualized bringing the characters to life on screen. Designers imagined what Pooh and Piglet costumes might look like and then actors at Disney World lived out caricatures of Pooh, Piglet, Tigger, and others to the delight of children visiting the theme park. Today, I creatively respond to the challenges of our nation's political scene by remembering wisdom embodied by a Small and Anxious Animal.

"Wow!" Piglet responded. "All that from a bedtime story."

"Double wow," I rejoined. "And to think that although you began as an idea in A.A. Milne's imagination, you've taken on a life of your own in the 100 Aker Wood and in the lives of children and their parents and grandparents! Just think of your own creativity. You imagine a gift for Eeyore and inspire a song for Winnie. You visualize how you can escape Owl's fallen tree to save Owl and Pooh."

"I never thought of a Small Animal as an artist and creator. But I guess I am. I'm creating every day. Because of that, everyday

can be exciting and adventurous. You begin the day walking with a friend and end up going on an Expotition to the North Pole!"

"And, Piglet, you've inspired me. I wouldn't be putting these words together, if I hadn't encountered you first nearly fifty years ago and re-discovered you in telling stories to my grandchildren."

"I didn't know that, but now I know that I'm always doing something new, even when I'm a little anxious. I AM a creator!"

"Yes, Piglet, and though you planned to go home if you saw a Heffalump in the Trap, you may decide to take another course of action. You may engage this strange creature in a conversation or go looking for Pooh or Christopher Robin to help you figure out what you're dealing with in the Trap. What happens next, no one can fully imagine, and it can change at any moment as a result of our decisions. The future is open and full of possibility."

Process theologians affirm that every moment of experience is a creative synthesis, joining past, present, and future; order and novelty; what has happened and what may emerge. We are meant to create, and we cannot help but to create regardless of our circumstances. Even God is constantly creating. I've repeated throughout this book the words of Lamentations:

The steadfast love of the Lord never ceases, his mercies never come to an end; they are new every morning; great is your faithfulness.

God is completely faithful. God's wisdom is reflected in the orderly movements of the planets and the seasons of the year. Still, God is constantly creating new possibilities. God is constantly doing new things to bring greater beauty into the universe. There are no dead ends in God's world, nor are there any dead ends in our lives. Even in the most tragic situations, we can still choose our response to what is happening to us or around us. Our past doesn't determine our present or future. That's really the theme of another book of stories, the Bible: God calls and human respond, and out of that dialogue new possibilities emerge. When the people go in the wrong direction, God must alter God's course to help them find the right way. Sometimes our decisions, like the decisions of the residents of Nineveh, described in the fable of Jonah, may even surprise God, and challenge God to change God's own mind.

"Jonah? Tell me about that. Weren't there stuffed animals in that story? A big fish and cattle?"

"Well, I don't exactly know the models the storyteller used, but even in the story of Jonah, who runs away from God, non-humans are creative. God whispers in the ear of a big fish who hunts Jonah down, swallows him but keeps him in a safe place in his body. Then, after all of Jonah's praying and complaining, the great fish spits the reluctant prophet out near the hated city of Nineveh. Talk about a creative fish! When Jonah preaches about a disaster coming, even the cattle take notice and go on a fast, along with their human owners. God calls and we respond, changing the world, and changing the course of God's action. God is always creative and God's creativity inspires our own creative attempts to bring goodness and beauty to the world."

"I guess if a big fish and a cow can be creative, then I can be creative, too" chirped Piglet. "I constantly remember that I am a Small Animal and that I am often quite anxious. But then I surprise myself. I go on an unexpected Expotition with Pooh and our friends. I climb a rope to save Pooh and Owl after his tree house blown down in a storm. I draft a letter to put in a bottle as the waters are rising around my own tree house. There's a lot I can't control, including my tendency to be anxious, but I don't have to let my anxiety get the best of me. That's when my creativity comes forth. That's when I do something I hadn't expected and end up saving the day!"

"Yes, Piglet, we always have a choice. I remember a doctor telling a young child who was afraid to go to bed because he had bad dreams, 'It's ok to be afraid, but you don't have to be afraid of being afraid.' What is that saying? 'Courage is fear that has said

its prayers'. In this moment, we can choose another path. We can change direction. We can use the past as the material for creating a new future. And that's being creative, whether a child learns to be brave in the dark or a nation learns how to beat its swords into plowshares and feed the poor rather than dropping bombs."

"So far Piglet, we've covered a lot of ground as theologians. We've claimed with the process theologians that experience is universal, that whatever experiences is valuable and deserves ethical consideration, and now that the more creative we are, the more alive we can be. In speaking of human destiny, an early Christian theologian stated that 'the glory of God is a fully alive human.' I wonder if that applies to Small and Anxious Animals, Rotund Bears, and Bouncing Tiggers. I wonder if God's glory is revealed in the creativity of artists, meandering Bears and their friends, toddlers playing with stuffed toys, and persons making the best of difficult situations."

Process theology sees creativity and artistry everywhere, and the quest for creative responses is most difficult in challenging times. Limits are constantly placed on us by our past and by the actions of others. Some of the limits, the realities that shape our lives, can be devastating. Children in Syria are waking up to bomb blasts. Other children are being treated for life-threatening illnesses in American hospitals. Parents feel hopeless as they imagine their child's future in a war-ravaged land or in facing day after day of medical treatments. But, even here there are moments of creativity. A child in the hospital room gains a moment of peace and comfort playing with a stuffed toy or watching a video about the adventures of Winnie the Pooh and his friends; a desperate parent reaches out to God in prayer or seeks the counsel of a dear friend; a safe and secure community decides to open its doors to Syrian refugees despite the fears that many residents have of strangers in their midst. All these are acts of creativity, all these bring something positive out of the wreckage of life. We can think small and be ruled by our fears, but Piglet reminds us that fear shouldn't keep us from doing the right thing.

"I've learned that I have to be bigger than my fears. I want to run away and go back to bed, but I know that I need to move forward, sometimes holding Pooh's hand, but go forward I must if I want to be of service. Creativity opens your mind and heart. That's what helped me give up my tree house so Owl could find a new home. I really didn't know I could, but then I remembered that Pooh was beside me, and that we could make a good life in his tree house, and off we went on new adventures."

"Creativity helps us find a way where it looks like there's no way forward. I remember a wise thinker, Victor Frankl, saying that they can take everything away from a person except her or his ability to respond in her or his own unique way to the circumstances of life. Some of the most free people have looked at the world through jail bars — I think of the Apostle Paul, John of the Cross, Nelson Mandela, Martin Luther King, Sojourner Truth, John McCain, and Mahatma Gandhi. People could put their bodies in prison, but their spirits soared! Regardless of what others did, they could claim, 'Free at last, free at last, God all-loving free at last'."

CHAPTER SIX

SMALL IS
BEAUTIFUL

"It is hard to be brave," Piglet sniffling slightly, when you're only a Very Small Animal."

Rabbit, who had begun to write very busily, looked up and said:

"It is because you are a very small animal that you will be Useful in the adventure before us."[10]

In the 100 Aker Wood, everyone matters. A small bug — known as "Small" — can inspire a search party. Little Piglet can be pivotal in an expedition and can save the day when Owl's house is blown down." Rabbit responds that "it is because you are small that you will be Useful in the adventure before us." Even though the ill-conceived adventure, involving substituting Piglet for Roo, becomes a misadventure, Piglet eventually becomes an essential actor in lowering the tensions between certain, somewhat xenophobic, residents of the 100 Aker Wood and the strange newcomers — Kanga and Roo — to the Wood.

Process theology recognizes the intricate interdependence of life. Nothing is inconsequential. Everything, even the smallest creature, matters to God and to us. The smallest action done by an apparently unimportant person can be over time a factor in a great result. The world is seldom transformed by one dramatic action, but by countless, seemingly unimportant decisions made one moment at a time. We are saved daily by the operation of microscopic

---

10   Ibid., 98.

T-cells and the survival of sea — and perhaps — land life depends on the abundance of small organisms, krill and plankton.

> *Looking over my shoulder as I typed, Piglet agreed. "Being small isn't easy and I have to work every day to remember my size doesn't determine the size of my heart. I can do great things even when I'm afraid: that's my daily affirmation. What would have happened to Owl and Pooh if I hadn't climbed through the mail slot or would Owl have found a home if I hadn't let him live in my tree house?"*

Today, proponents of chaos theory speak of the significance of the butterfly effect as a model for the power of small deviations to lead to great changes in weather patterns. According to meteorologist Edward Lorenz, very small changes in the initial conditions leading up to an event can lead to significantly different outcomes. For example, a monarch butterfly, flapping its wings in Pacific Grove, California, near where I grew up, can play a significant role in the blustery winds I experienced this morning as walked along Craigville Beach on Cape Cod, Massachusetts. It's not about size; it's about connection and impact.

The affirmation of the importance of small things is at the heart of Jesus' good news. In describing God's realm of Shalom — of peace and justice for all creation — Jesus gives this parable:

> *He put before them another parable: "The kingdom of heaven is like a mustard seed that someone took and sowed in his field; it is the smallest of all the seeds, but when it has grown it is the greatest of shrubs and becomes a tree, so that the birds of the air come and make nests in its branches."* (Matthew 13:31-32)

A little scientific research tells us that mustard seed is not the smallest of seeds, but Jesus' parable — like the scripture as a whole — isn't about science, it's about spirituality. Mustard seeds are contagious. I know this for a fact. As a young boy, I wanted to test Jesus' words. I planted a mustard seed in our backyard. Soon, a mustard plant emerged and shortly thereafter another burst forth and then one more, until my mother cut them down, fearing they would take over the whole back yard.

Another gospel passage reports that when the disciples asked Jesus to increase their faith, he responded: "If you had faith the size of a mustard seed, you could say to this mulberry tree, 'Be uprooted and planted in the sea,' and it would obey you." (Luke 17:6) Once again, something small can be pivotal in transforming our lives. Trusting God's power in our lives can be the tipping point, even with all our doubts and insecurities, moving us from fear to love and impotence to activism. This was the case with Rosa Parks, whose choice to stay in her seat in violation of a local ordinance, was catalytic in the American civil rights movement. One woman, sitting on a bus, can change the nation. This same catalytic spirituality was at work when a young boy brought his five loaves and two fish to Jesus, enabling Jesus to feed a crowd of five thousand. We don't know how this miracle occurred: Did Jesus morph a morsel into a smorgasbord by assessing the primal energy of the universe? Or, did the boy's act of generosity inspire the rest of the crowd to open their satchels to share their lunches? Regardless of the explanation we favor, the loaves and fish were multiplied — a small act led to a great result.

If Jesus had been aware of contemporary cosmology, he might have chosen the initial moment of the big bang to describe the realm of God. From a singularity — infinitely small, infinitely hot, and infinitely dense — our universe of billions of galaxies emerged. Small can be breathtaking in its ultimate impact.

In describing the spiritual journey of persons and planets, Jewish mystics proclaim that when you save a soul, you save the world. At first, that's hard to believe. One soul saved out of billions isn't much, and can't possibly make a difference, says the realist. But mystics see deeper than realists: they recognize that the world cannot be saved unless every soul realizes its true nature, the divine light within. Accordingly, as insignificant as it may seem, your impact on the person with whom you are interacting today is pivotal to the future well-being of our planet.

As a child, I often heard preachers describe the parable of the lost sheep as an example of God's compassion for wayward souls, and it surely is. God loves every lost sheep — or Piglet — and will spend all night searching for it. But, there is more to the story than the rescue of one lost sheep. The good shepherd leaves the ninety nine sheep not only to save the lost one, but to save the ninety nine. They cannot be complete without the hundredth. They cannot be saved until every lost soul is healed and welcomed home. They need the hundredth sheep as much as she needs them.

Always sensitive to others' feelings, Piglet cautiously noted, "You seem a little distracted today. What's going on? You aren't bouncing around like Tigger."

"Oh, so you noticed," I replied, "You see, beyond the Wood in the bigger world, we've inaugurated a new president and I'm worried about our nation's future. I think we're entering a dark time, and I don't know what to do."

"Oh, we've heard about the goings on beyond the Wood, and wonder how they will change the lives of stuffed toys and children and the Wood — beauty and imagination doesn't seem to matter to many politicians these days. But, don't give up hope. Remember that today people remember Jesus and not Herod. Just do your part. Be faithful, do the right thing, and save the part of the world where you are. That can move mountains."

"Thanks, Piglet, you're small, but you may have changed my life today. It's what I call the George Bailey Principle from the film, 'It's a Wonderful Life.' George thought his life was a failure until he discovered how different the world would have been if he'd never been born. A whole town would have been plunged into darkness, lives would have been lost in hopelessness and poverty, and one woman would never have found true love. We can't always be successful, but we can be faithful, and our faith can move mountains."

*"That's the spirit, Bruce," Piglet affirmed. "When we face the
mountains of our lives and 'blinch' a little, we can still be brave.
Small creatures can make a difference on a big stage. After all,
people are still talking about me!"*

Yes, small makes a difference. The philosopher Whitehead says
the whole universe conspires to create each moment of experience,
and each moment of experience radiates beyond itself, shaping even
what God can do. Each small moment is our gift to the universe,
expanding or contracting the range of possibility for its successors.
We can drop our pebble in the pond, not knowing the ultimate
impact of our act, but be confident as we see the ripples that the
world is vastly different simply because we were here and did our
part at this moment in time.

CHAPTER SEVEN

ADVENTURE AROUND
EVERY CORNER

"Oh, Piglet," Pooh said excitedly, "we're going on an Expotition, all of us, with things to eat. To discover something."

"To discover what? Piglet said anxiously.

"Oh! Just something."

"Nothing fierce?"

Process theology is an adventure of ideas. More than that, process theology is an invitation to intellectual, spiritual, relational, and community adventures. The pure conservative, seeking to hang onto the way things were in business or the church or to make our nation great again by going back to the 1950s, is going against the grain of the universe. In fact, he or she may be going against the ever-flowing streams of divine creativity. Life goes forward, building on the past, but leaning toward new possibilities. Along the way, many paths are presented to us, each beckoning us to choose our own adventures.

The Bible is an adventure book. The children of Israel are constantly on the move. They constantly must adapt to the social, political, and economic realities of their time. Faithfulness to God involves embracing change when we discover that yesterday's solutions no longer work. Beneath the people's adventures is an adventurous God of wind and storm, of mountain and wilderness, who is constantly doing a new thing and urging God's faithful to embrace novelty as well.

Jesus of Nazareth was an adventurer as well. Discontent with the religion of his time, Jesus called a small community of women and men to become residents of God's coming realm through acts of hospitality and fidelity. Jesus invited his followers to launch out into deep waters with assurance that God was with them. As long as they kept their eyes on him, they would do what they previously imagined as impossible.

For Jesus, no written book or law was ever final. Jesus asked his followers to experience God as a living and loving presence in themselves and in the world, bringing forth great harvests from small beginnings. Our lives are holy adventures, Jesus taught, whether they involve travel to unfamiliar shores and peregrinations in our local community. No two moments are the same, and no two encounters are ever the same. All life calls us to creativity and creativity inspires adventure.

"Life in the Wood is an adventure," Piglet chipped in. "Sometimes we choose to go on an adventure not knowing where it will lead. The other day we went looking for the North Pole. I was worried that we might encounter something fierce — a Woozle or a Heffalump. Winnie the Pooh just found a pole beside our path, and we celebrated the discovery. We weren't sure what the North Pole would be like till we found it."

"Yes, Piglet, on the adventure, we don't usually know what we'll find. We just know that there's something more out there to be found. Sometimes adventurers end up far from where they expected. On the way to India, they discover the Americas, and then a whole new set of adventures emerges. A few years back my goal was to be a seminary dean or president and I ended up as a 'wash ashore' village pastor on Cape Cod! And, I've never been happier!"

"The Wood isn't large, only 100 acres, but it's full of surprises," Piglet added.

"Adventure is both the nature of life, the way the universe works bringing forth new possibilities and presenting varieties of

solutions to challenges. It is also an attitude of mind. Alfred North Whitehead talks about adventures of ideas. Great ideas emerge for those who are willing to explore new ways of looking at the world. You don't have to leave your study or backyard to have an adventure. I think of my young grandchildren, who create small universes with their Legos or can imagine a stuffed toy as a superhero embarking on a perilous quest. When I was a boy, I created whole countries and baseball leagues in my bedroom and backyard. To the adventurous mind, a grain of sand can reveal a hidden universe and every day is a heroic journey. It's all about asking 'what's next?' and then embracing what comes your way.

Process theologians believe that we live in an adventurous universe. Hurtling at breakneck speed from an energetic burst some fourteen billion years ago, the universe is incomplete and unfinished, and its future pathways are uncertain. Life is even an adventure for God, as the scriptures assert. God doesn't have everything determined in advance. Novelty happens to God too. At least that's what the tale of Jonah suggests. God's initial plan is to tell the people of Nineveh that their great city will be devastated as a result of their violence and immorality. But, then, when the people change their ways, God changes God's mind and the city is spared. The future is open for God and for us. If everything is decided or known in advance in some sort of eternal vision, then nothing new happens, just the same thing over and over, for God and us.

"That's right," Piglet chimed in. "I feel anxious when something unexpected happens. But I also feel alive and thrilled at what might happen next. I'm glad nothing's entirely predictable in the Wood. Eeyore always complains and Rabbit always organizes, but then Tigger bounces in, upsetting their plans. Winnie the Pooh is always thinking of honey, but sometimes he stalks the bees and other times, the bees chase him."

"I'm so glad, Piglet, that we can take this adventure together.

"So am I," responded my Small and Sometimes Anxious Companion.

CHAPTER EIGHT

WE WALK
IN BEAUTY

*[Pooh] left Rabbit and hurried down to Piglet's house. Piglet
was sitting on the ground at the door of his house blowing happily
on a dandelion, and wondering whether it would be this year, next
year, sometime or never.*

A few years ago, my wife and I moved back to Washington
DC to support our son's family following the birth of our second
grandson. This one-year adventure led to my reflections on the
Gospel According to Winnie the Pooh and *Piglet's Process*. We had
moved from bucolic Lancaster, Pennsylvania, where I had served
as professor and seminary administrator, to the hustle and bustle
of Friendship Heights, just a block over the border from Washington DC. Instead of a woodland home, we found ourselves living
on the eighteenth floor of a grand apartment building with over
two thousand residents, a store, and a restaurant. Our apartment
building was tucked among a sea of other high-rise buildings just
a block away from Wisconsin Avenue, one the busiest avenues in
our nation's capital. Yet, just a few hundred yards from our high
rise, I discovered a stream and an acre plot that my oldest grandson
and I named the One Acre Wood. We had just begun reading
the Winnie the Pooh stories in abbreviated form, and he loved the
creatures of the 100 Aker Wood. It was a beauty spot, a quiet glade,
where a two-year old and his grandfather could spin out tales of
Winnie the Pooh and other toddler imaginings.

Nearly every afternoon, I would pack up my grandson's stroller
with some treats I'd packed and we would head to the One Aker
Wood to take little hikes, listen to the stream, and play games. His
imagination roamed free and so did mine as we toddled in this

postage stamp forest. A book was born in those meanderings and from this first book, this little sibling, Piglet's reflections on process theology, has emerged.

We found that you don't need a hundred acres of woodlands or a picturesque shoreline to experience beauty. Beauty can be discovered in the most unexpected places — in a flower pot on the eighteenth floor of an urban high rise, in a photo of a grandchild, in the face of an elder, in snowflakes falling, in sunsets and sunrises, and in our own daily peregrinations. As the first Americans of the Southwest proclaim, "with beauty all around me I walk." We respond, as we open our eyes to holiness everywhere, "with beauty all around us we walk."

> "I like that story, professor," chimed in Piglet. "I've only seen pictures of cities, but I can imagine a little beauty spot just off the beaten track. I can imagine something that no one else notices but a little boy and his grandfather."

> "I bet most people are too busy to notice the 100 Aker Wood, Piglet, and that may be a good thing, given our tendency to sacrifice beauty for utility. I suspect a few business people imagine the Wood as an upscale housing development for commuters into London and miss the simple beauty of woods and meadow and stream. You know that song, 'pave paradise and put up a parking lot.' Beauty can be all around, but only those who pause to notice, will see it and be forever changed."

> "Beauty is here — in something as temporary as a dandelion — and you can overlook it if you don't pause awhile and open your eyes and blow on it," Piglet responded.

> "That's the beauty of beauty, Piglet. It seldom lasts forever. Yes, there are the Rockies and Nantucket Sound, the Grand Canyon and the Barrier Reef. They will outlive us, but it is just for a moment that we delight in them, and some beauties like your dandelion are here in this moment and gone the next."

The first American settlers were right — beauty surrounds us wherever we are. The heavens declare the glory of God and so do gentle breezes, lapping waves, purple flowers, and mountaintops. God's glory fills our senses and we can experience it in the face of a child or senior adult, the smell of a rose or a good meal, and in the taste of a well-crafted lasagna or freshly made ice cream.

The whole universe, as the philosopher Alfred North White-head asserted, is aimed at the production of beauty. We live in a beautiful universe full of contrasts and novelty. We gaze at photos from the Hubble telescope and are transfixed by cosmic beauty — of swirling galaxies, of supernovas, of bits of color bursting forth in "empty space." The cosmos is a tapestry of divine artistry and so is the wondrous universe hidden in our circulatory and immune systems, in firing neurons, and the harmony of body, mind, and spirit.

For process theologians, beauty is a moral category. It involves affirming contrast, diversity, and change. Beauty welcomes strangers and never stands still. God loves beauty and wants us to be partners in preserving and creating the beauty that surrounds us. The universe is an aesthetic adventure embodied billions of times each millisecond in bringing together the many elements of experience, taken from the environment and immediate past, into one unique experience each moment of the day. This is true not only among those designated as artists, writers, and creators but in the experience of every child and adult. Yes, we make beautiful things — the Pyramids, the skyline of Manhattan, a Bach fugue and Pachelbel's canon, the Mona Lisa and Falling Waters — and we should celebrate them because they are part of that Greater Beauty toward which the Poet of the Universe lures us.

The famed physician, musician, and Bible scholar Albert Schweitzer once described "reverence for life" as the primary ethical value. Process theologians would add that reverence for life inspires us to add beauty to the universe by our day to day actions. We must not, theologians of beauty declare, deface the beauty of the universe. We must, as process theologian Patricia Adams Farmer counsels, embrace a beautiful God and become beautiful in the process.

Ordinary things can be done lovingly in ways that add beauty to life. Mother Teresa captured the same sentiment when she counseled, "Do something beautiful for God!" Her namesake Thérèse of Lisieux counseled, "Do little things with great love!" The two saints, Therese and Theresa, remind us that our lives can be a work of art, contributing to the beauty of the world. She recognized that acts of service and compassion can bring a moment's beauty even to dying persons.

> *"You mean a honey pot can be beautiful?" Piglet queried.*

> *"Well, it's not exactly a van Gogh, but the very experience of golden honey, pierced by sunlight and the smooth, sweet taste can be beautiful."*

> *"Even dandelions and red balloons, right? But, what about that red balloon that popped just as I was bringing it to Eeyore's party. That can be beautiful?"*

> *"Yes, even that, Piglet. There can be beauty of spirit and beauty of generosity just as there can be beauty of human artistry and natural landscapes and seascapes. Beauty's all around, and those you notice, say 'Awe' and give thanks."*

Process theologians affirm God's aim at beauty. Divine wisdom seeks to bring forth beauty over the long haul of evolution. Pain exists and creatures are often at cross purposes in their quest for survival and flourishing, but still there is an inner movement toward beauty. As the most moved mover, the One who knows every celebration and heartache, God feels the pain of creation. Had the universe remained at the cellular level and never evolved, there would have been minimal pain and conflict but also only a teaspoon full of beauty. But God's own patient evolving of creation brought forth the possibility of beauty beyond our imaginations as well as the pain of conflict and disease. God bears the pain of the world; and God rejoices in the wonder of life.

> *"Life is pretty good here in the Wood. Sometimes I know that there is conflict and, of course, Eeyore carries the burdens of the world on his shoulders. But I try to bring something lovely into his life — a balloon, a flower, a new place to live — and I know that Eeyore experiences silver linings in his dark clouds." Piglet noted.*

> *"Beauty matters, and even the smallest act can bring beauty to those around you and to the universe in its totality. That's why you brought that balloon to Eeyore!" I replied.*

Process theologians believe that we have a choice and the future of the world may hinge on our choices: Will our actions add or subtract from the beauty of life? They also ask us to consider: Will our actions give God a more beautiful or uglier world with which to interact? Our lives are works of art, and in seeking beauty, we bring greater beauty to the world around us and to God's experience of the world. With beauty all around us, we walk. With hearts open to beauty, we bring beauty to others. We do something beautiful for God, even in the darkest moments of life. We join God's quest to birth beauty wherever we go.

CHAPTER NINE

FAT SOUL
SPIRITUALITY

"And there Piglet is," said Owl, "If the string doesn't break."

"Supposing it does," asked Piglet.

"Then we try another piece of string."

This was not very comforting to Piglet because however many pieces of string they tried pulling up with, it would always be the same him coming down; but still, it seemed like the only thing to do. So with one last look back in his mind at all the happy hours he had spent in the Forest not being pulled up to the ceiling by a piece of string, Piglet nodded bravely at Pooh and said that it was a Very Clever pup-pup-pup Clever pup-pup Plan.[11]

Process theology believes that our experiences of beauty increase our spiritual size. We become larger persons when we can embrace complexity and contrast and when we can appreciate diversity of sounds, viewpoints, and persons. We become, as process theologian Patricia Farmer says, fat souls.

"That's interesting," interjected Piglet. "When I think of a fat soul, I think of Winnie the Pooh and his love for honey. He'll go anywhere and try anything to have a smackerel of honey. I remember the time when he had so much honey at rabbit's house that he couldn't squeeze through Rabbit's front door. He was sure a fat soul, or rather, a fat belly!"

"Well, Piglet, it is about size but the size I'm thinking about involves our relationships and spiritual life. It involves how much

---

11 Ibid., 323.

diversity you can take in without losing your way. How much of others' experiences you can affirm while still following our own path."

"Oh, I get it. I grow in size — I get bigger inside — when I feel afraid but still do something brave or when I let owl live in my tree house because he needs a place to stay. I felt bad at first, but then I felt really good, because I wasn't worried about holding on to my familiar place but could live anywhere."

One of my favorite scriptures describes Jesus growing "in wisdom and stature and favor with God and humanity." (Luke 2:52, my adaptation) Having a fat soul is about growing in spirit, not just your waistline. It's about welcoming newcomers and learning from people who are different than you. It's about embracing new ways of thinking and new perspectives on life.

"Piglet, do you remember when Kanga and Roo first moved to the forest. Rabbit and some of the forest dwellers were concerned that these Strange Animals with unusual habits would change the Wood. Rabbit didn't think they would fit in and that the best thing to do would be to get them to go back where they came from, wherever that was. He wanted things to stay the way they were. So he devised a plan, but it really failed, didn't it?"

"Yes, I was part of the plan. I had nothing against Kanga and Roo, or newcomers to the Wood. I just got caught up in Rabbit's anxiety and suddenly I found myself in Kanga's pouch, jostled this way and that as she hopped through the Wood. She really fooled me. She acted like I was Roo and gave me a bath — yuk! — and medicine, too. Luckily, Rabbit got to know Roo and soon they became the best of friends."

"You discovered that strangers weren't threats. In fact, you found out that they added beauty and excitement to the Wood. That's stature, that's letting your fat soul grow to embrace others, especially when they are different than you."

"And Kanga had size and stature, too. She didn't get mad or go away, she played a joke on me, and everyone ended up being friends. I like the idea of welcoming strangers and new things in my life. As a Small Animal, I often become anxious. When Pooh and Owl asked me to climb out of the fallen tree, at first, all I thought about was falling, but then I took a deep breath and visualized myself climbing, and off I went. I don't think I'm a hero, but I saved the day!"

"Yes, Piglet, you're right. The more we can accept of ourselves and others, the bigger our souls are. In America, a long way from the Wood, a lot of people can't deal with difference. They don't like people who come from other countries and persons from other religions frighten them. They think that friendship depends of being alike, believing the same things, and watching the same news programs. Some of them can't even imagine welcoming newcomers to the country. They see them as a threat to their religion and way of life."

"Well, I learned my lesson with Kanga and Roo and Tigger. We are bigger and better when we welcome other creatures to the Wood. We are more creative when we sing new songs and walk new paths. It's a stretch at times, but once you get over your fear, a new world opens up and everyday becomes an adventure."

To process thinkers, big souls are beautiful souls and beautiful souls are lively souls. God is the biggest, fattest, most spacious soul because God embraces everyone. As the song says, God's "got the whole world in God's hands." God embraces friends and enemies, galaxies and cells, and delights in all the colors of the rainbow. That's the fat soul ethic: be like God, have a large soul, and embrace the world with love.

CHAPTER TEN

SOUL
FRIENDS

*Christopher Robin had a question to ask first, and he won-
dered how to ask it.*

*"Well," he said at last, "It's a very nice house, and if your
own house is blown down, you must go somewhere else, mustn't
you, Piglet? What would you do if your house was blown down?"*

Before Piglet could think, Pooh answered for him.

*"He'd come and live with me," said Pooh, "wouldn't you,
Piglet?"*

Piglet squeezed his paw.

"Thank you, Pooh," he said, "I should love to."[12]

Pooh understood something that often eludes political and
business leaders: none of us is self-made; we become what we are
meant to be through positive and supportive relationships. That's
not only an interpersonal reality but the heart of the universe. We
are all related and when we claim the Graceful Interdependence of
Beloved Communities, we are always home.

Celtic spirituality describes the relational nature of life in terms
anamcara or soul friendship. The Celtic sages believed that we
flourish when we have one person who mirrors our soul and in
whose eyes we see the face of God. Just as the Celts spoke of "thin
places," where heaven and earth meet and divine inspiration is
revealed in woodlands, stones, meadows, and waves, they also rec-

---

12 Ibid., 341.

ognized that God meets us in our relationships with other persons. As we experience the beauty of another person, we are reminded of the Beauty that is at the heart of creation and we are inspired to seek Beauty everywhere. Your *anamcara* is the person with whom you can be fully yourself in your grandeur and foolishness. A person without a spiritual friend is like a boat without a rudder, drifting without purpose or direction, so asserted the Celtic spiritual guides. Your *anamcara* brings forth the holiness — and the healing needed — in yourself and the one who is your beloved friend.

The notion of *anamcara*, or salvation through relationship, is global. Martin Luther King spoke of the healing power of relationships as a fabric of connections in which I cannot be who I am intended to be until you are who you are intended to be. In South Africa, the word *Ubuntu* was coined to describe this same unity of life, often embodied in particular relationships, but intended to characterize the relationships of communities which share a common ground and empathy among their members. Broadly speaking, *Ubuntu* means "a person is a person through other people."

> *"This is getting pretty philosophical,"* Piglet averred, *"even for process theology. But, beneath the words, it's simply love, isn't it? Making love the highest value and partnership the goal of life in the Wood. It's me and Pooh walking together through the Wood, and it's the two of us going on adventures and pursuing dreams. It's Christopher Robin and Pooh talking about the future in an enchanted place and vowing to remember each other regardless of what the future brings."*

> *"You're blessed to have a friend like Pooh. When you gave up your home to Owl, Pooh came forward and offered you a place in his home. You and Pooh toddle around together not knowing what's next but knowing that you will together come what may. Even when the idea of encountering a Woozle makes you feel anxious, you know that with Pooh and Christopher Robin, no Woozle can harm you."*

"I wouldn't be me without Pooh," Piglet replied. "And Pooh needs me to be his companion as he seeks honey, Heffalumps, and Woozles."

Process theology is all about relationships. Our relationships are ingredients from which our lives emerge. Our relationships provide us with the inspiration, energy, and texture from which we create our own experiences. We are all connected, and spiritual friendships — like the Celtic *anamcara* — heal our spirits and show us the way. Even the most independent persons need a supportive environment to flourish.

"Pooh and I are anamcara -friends, aren't we?" Piglet ventured.

"Yes, you are different but your souls are in synch. You mirror each other's hopes and respond to each other's needs. You have a deep knowing about how to help the other become his best. Anamcara, spiritual friends forever, and Ubuntu, celebrating our relationships, that's what brings light to our lives and love to our hearts."

"Piglet, I know you haven't ever been out of the Wood, but I know that you can see greatness when you encounter it. A great spiritual leader, South African Desmond Tutu, spoke of Ubuntu, a type of soul friendship that characterizes a whole community this way —'a person with Ubuntu is open and available to others, affirming of others, does not feel threatened that others are able and good, based from a proper self-assurance that comes from knowing that he or she belongs in a greater whole and is diminished when others are humiliated or diminished, when others are tortured or oppressed....One of the sayings in our country is Ubuntu — the essence of being human. Ubuntu speaks particularly about the fact that you can't exist as a human being in isolation. It speaks about our interconnectedness. You can't be human all by yourself, and when you have this quality — Ubuntu — you are known for your generosity. We think of ourselves far too frequently as just individuals, separated from one another, whereas you are connected and

what you do affects the whole World. When you do well, it spreads out; it is for the whole of humanity.' Piglet, whether we call this process theology, unbuntu, or anamcara, it simply means we are one, and we need to recognize and act on our unity."

"That's what it's like in the Wood, I think," Piglet responded. "We're all unique and sometimes quirky, but there's a place for each of us in the whole community. Orderly Rabbit needs boundless Tigger to add zest to life and Tigger needs Kanga to slow himself down. Despondent Eeyore needs hopeful Pooh. Wise Old Owl needs someone to talk to — anyone it seems! Pooh and I can't go on an adventure without each other's company. We all need Christopher Robin to bring us to life and he needs us to go on an Expotition. It takes a village to truly be ourselves here in the Wood."

"Yes, we're all related, Piglet. We just don't recognize it. But when we realize how much we matter to each other, whether as special spiritual friends or life companions or simply fellow citizens, our hearts swell and our souls become fat, and the whole world becomes a Beloved Community."

Process theologians assert that we need soul friendship or Ubuntu now more than ever not only among close friends, but on a planetary level. Too many persons think they can go it alone; they see self-interest as the key to happiness. Too many nations think they can go it alone; they want to build walls, keep out strangers, and stop the flow of creative ideas. They forget that no person or nation is an island, and that even the strongest nation requires other nations for its well-being.

The Grace of Interdependence, God's energetic and relational presence in all things, needs to be our inspiration as we build cities, grow crops, plan our personal and national priorities, and look toward the future of the planet. We need a sense of reverence for life, as Albert Schweitzer asserted, that includes woodlands, streams, oceans, mountains, and meadows as well as well as our fellow humans and animal companion. The experience of awe at the birth of a child must also inspire our sense of wonder as we view dolphins leaping and osprey migrating. In seeing Beauty in the face of your beloved companion, we are inspired to experience — and then bring forth — beauty everywhere. In that fragile and lively Graceful Interdependence, we are all one, and that One Life courses through us, energizing, inspiring, and uniting for the Common Good — to save the Wood and save the planet.

CHAPTER ELEVEN

EARTHLY
GOOD

*"Just the house for Owl. Don't you think so, little Piglet,"[said
Eeyore] And then Piglet did a Noble Thing, and he did it in sort of
a dream, while he was thinking of all the wonderful words Pooh
had hummed about him.*

*"Yes, it's just the house for Owl," he said grandly. "I hope he
will be very happy in it." And then he gulped twice, because he
had been very happy in it himself.*[13]

Back in the small town where I grew up, certain people were
described as "so heavenly minded that they are no earthly good."
The comment was intended to portray the "saints" whose prayer
lives rendered them useless in responding to challenges of everyday
life. In contrast, process theology affirms that our calling is to be
both "heavenly minded and earthly good." By that, I mean that
spiritual maturity involves experiencing God's presence in everyday life by seeking to do something beautiful for God in every
encounter. The world is chock-full with divinity. "Thin places"
where heaven and earth meet are everywhere. With the Roman
Catholic mystic Thérèse of Lisieux, we can do ordinary things with
great love.

*"I love to look at the scudding clouds and listen to the bab-
bling brook," observed Piglet. "Sometimes I just want to spend the
day daydreaming and lounging about with Pooh. But, a good day
also involves caring for my friends in the 100 Aker Wood. I feel
great energy and power when I bring a gift to Eeyore, climb a rope
to save Pooh and Owl despite my fears, and give up my tree house*

---

so Owl can have a place to live. I like looking at the stars, but my inspiration always brings me back to the Wood and the joys and problems of my friends there."

"I'm with you, Piglet. I love the life of the mind. There's nothing I'd rather do than spend a day writing, walking on the beach, and quietly meditating. But, what joy I feel when I visit a patient at the hospital, feed the hungry at the soup kitchen, hammer nails for Habitat for Humanity, or play with my grand-children. Life is a yin-yang. We rest and then we act. We pray and then we protest. We meditate and then we hit the streets to help the homeless."

"Prof, these words warm the heart of a Small Animal. I remember Christopher Robin talking about a woman who worked on the streets of Calcutta in India, way beyond the wood. She said that she wanted to do something beautiful for God. I don't know much about God, but I want to do something beautiful. I want to leave a path of beauty wherever I walk in the Wood."

"Yes, dear Piglet. Something beautiful for God, that's what Mother Teresa said. Love the Wood, rejoice in silence, take time to play, but also pray when you walk, when you serve breakfast to your family, when you call your political leaders. I remember a motto on a bench at the Kirkridge Retreat Center in Pennsylvania that counseled us to 'picket and pray.'"

Picket and pray! Do something beautiful for God! Do ordinary things with great love! That's the heart of process theology. We need to reflect, but we also must remember that our lives are our gifts to God. Whatever we do on earth ripples toward the heavens. Every act creates a field of force that brings beauty or ugliness or healing or separation to our environment.

Jesus once said, "Your kingdom come, your will be done, on earth as it is in heaven." I think he meant that we should always have our eyes on heaven — we should be heavenly-minded. But this is not escape from the world. We want to bring our spiritual insights to daily life. If we discover God's presence in all things, then we need to do everything we can to make the world a better place. We want the world to mirror God's vision of Shalom, of love, justice, and healing. We want earth to look like heaven. God gives us a vision of love for every encounter and when we let God's vision guide us, we bring beauty to the earth.

By being earthly good, we bring beauty to both heaven and earth. We give God a beautiful world. We give God more love and beauty, and help God be more present in our world. When we turn to God, we help God's vision come alive where we are. We create a circle of love in which God can be more effective in changing hearts, minds, and hands.

CHAPTER TWELVE

PROVIDENCE
GENTLY MOVES

When Eeyore saw the pot [which Pooh gave him for his birthday], he became quite excited.

"Why," he said, "I believe my balloon will just go in that Pot!"

"Oh, no, Eeyore," said Pooh, "Balloons are much too big to go into Pots. What you do with the balloon, you hold the balloon."

"Not mine," said Eeyore proudly, "Look, Piglet!" And as Piglet looked sorrowfully round, Eeyore picked the balloon up with his teeth, and placed it carefully in the pot, picked it up and put it on the ground; and then picked it up again and put it carefully back.

"So it does!" said Pooh, "It goes in!"

"So it does!" said Piglet, "And it comes out!"

"Doesn't it?" said Eeyore. "It goes in and out like anything."[14]

We haven't talked much about God so far and that may surprise some readers who believe that any theological system should invoke God's name often and explicitly. Process theology is God-centered and surely as God-centered as those theologies that claim to be orthodox in their affirmation that God omnipotently guides the universe, choosing by divine fiat health and illness, life and death, saved and unsaved, war and peace, storm and calm. Process theol-

---

14 Ibid., 90.

ogy takes a different turn from those who believe that every event comes directly from the hand of God and that God coercively guides the stars, planets, and human life.

For process theologians, God is best described as the Gentle Providence, moving, for the most part, subtly and quietly through all things, constantly providing possibilities and the energy to embody them. For process theologians, omnipresence is a practical reality. You can't be a "little" omnipresent. Rather, God is in all things as the quiet force aiming at beauty, justice, community, and creativity. God's Gentle Providence guides, but does not compel, loves but does not control, and treasures but does not coerce. God is the reality in whom we live and move and have our being, such that we can affirm "God in all things, all things in God."

"I sense Something in my life that is more than the Wood," Piglet affirmed. "I feel a Presence in the wind that whips through the enchanted grove of trees, the bubbling waters of the creek, the warmth of the sun on a picnic with friends, and the bright full moon that guides our nighttime adventures."

"Yes, Piglet, you are right. God is present whether or not we notice. God is in the air we breathe, in every heartbeat, and in every act of compassion and kindness. God doesn't put up billboards and seldom announces God's presence, but God is here nevertheless. I felt God's presence in your generosity to Eeyore and even though the balloon popped, God was the inspiration for your gift and Eeyore's joy in receiving it. I saw God's hand in your generosity in providing a home for Owl and in Pooh's invitation for you to be his housemate. In every moment, God calls and invites us to respond with grace, love, generosity, and care."

"Do you think God is present in our daily lives in the Wood, Professor?"

"Once again, I say 'yes.' I think God invited Christopher Robin and the gang to go on an Expotition to the North Pole and then discover that the North Pole, the place of our searching,

is everywhere. I think God inspired Rabbit to go beyond his fear and become good friends with Roo. I think God is in the woodland creatures' constant kindness to the morose and curmudgeonly Eeyore."

Process theologians know that lots of people want a God who controls everything and ensures that "our side" wins. A lot of people want certainty and so they talk about God defeating their opponents, defending their land, and coming again to set everything right at the end of history. But a god who controls everything also plants the cancer cell, seeds the tornado, energizes the tidal wave, and blesses the oppressor's action. God, then, becomes as much a devil as a divinity.

Process theologians see God in terms of Gentle Providence. God never gives up, always supports, constantly inspires, and moment by moment challenges us to be God's companions in healing the world. God has a vision, but not an agenda. God's vision is beauty, God's action is loving, and God wants us to live out God's vision and action in our own unique ways. Like a good parent, God encourages greater freedom and creativity congruent with the well-being of the Whole. God wants us to create, take responsibility, and shape the contours of our lives. We can't live apart from God's guidance and energy, but this energy of love seeks to empower and not imprison. God even likes our surprises and supports our actions bring about something God hasn't fully expected.

Process theologians believe God is the "most moved mover." In contrast to the Greek philosopher Aristotle's vision of God dwelling in unchanging and unmoved splendor, process theologians see God as "new every morning" as well as faithful in every season of life. God is constantly doing new things and God is constantly experiencing new things. God feels our joy and sorrow, rejoicing in our success and empathizing with our pain.

"You mean God was with us on the Expotition to the North Pole? And, God was with us when I climbed that rope to save Owl and Pooh?"

"Yes, Piglet, God gave you a little push to help you save your friends. God knew you were anxious, and so God helped you imagine climbing the rope — all the way — and then heroically saving your friends. God rejoiced in your bravery and delighted in your generosity."

"Then, what we do truly matters to God," Piglet asserted.

"Yes, my friend. God is, as the philosopher Whitehead said, the fellow sufferer who understands. God is also the companion who rejoices in our success. God embraces everything that happens and tries to bring something good over the long haul out of even the most difficult situations. God is the heart and soul of the universe whose providence seeks beauty and love in all things."

"I don't see God, but now I know that I feel God in what is best in me and my friends. I am happy to know that God knows me and feels what a Small Animal feels. How good it is to know that I can do something helpful to God when I help my woodland neighbors."

"Yes, God even needs Small Animals. Small is beautiful and when a Small Animal is brave and generous, he brings beauty to the world and to the Creator."

God is the holy adventurer, the poet of the world, whose Gentle Providence moves through every creature and every moment. We are never alone. We are known by God, inspired by God, and loved by God, and in return we love this good earth, bringing beauty to one another and to our Companion and Adventurer.

CHAPTER THIRTEEN

WALKING EACH
OTHER HOME

"What do you like doing best in the world?" [Christopher Robin asked Winnie the Pooh.]....

"What I like best in the world is Me and Piglet going to see You, and You saying, 'What about a little something?' and me saying, 'Well, I shouldn't mind a little something, should you, Piglet,' and it being a hummy sort of day outside, and birds singing."[15]

We are meant for relationship. Even God needs relationships. That's the heart of the process vision. While many of us, including me, prize solitude for study, prayer, and reflection, our lives find richness in being part of a beloved community, whether this community consists of family, a few close friends, a congregation, or a village.

Within the 100 Aker Wood, relationships involve movement. While there are times that Pooh and his friends lounge around a honey pot speculating about what the day will bring, most of their time is spent meandering through the woodlands, synchronously encountering each other, and then going off together in pursuit of the adventures each day brings.

My closest friend once sent me a paper weight with the words, *solvitur ambulando,* "it will be solved in the walking." She knew that I loved walking. She also knew that physical and spiritual movement are intimately connected. When our bodies are moving, new ideas flood our minds and creative ideas often inspire us to make changes in our environment. My friend has passed away, but every time I see those words, I know that she's still with me —

---

15   Ibid., 352.

quietly guiding, because love lasts forever. Even death can't break the connection. Loving relationships endure forever.

The world we live in is far from complete. Its future is in doubt. Polar ice caps melt and waters rise on Cape Cod. Politicians send sophomoric tweets while bombs fall on civilians and children starve. As business people disregard prophets to focus on profits, even the 100 Aker Wood is in danger. Just down the road from the Wood, a housing development is being planned. Could the Wood be next as humans choose comfort and convenience over beauty and sustainability? Will Christopher Robin, and the Christopher Robin in each of us, remember places of youthful enchantment and come to the rescue of our youthful enchanted places before it's too late?

Once destroyed, beauty spots and species — and dare we say this good Earth — will never return. The Garden will be gone forever, the Wood give way to brick and mortar. Human artifice is also beautiful, but human creativity finds its proper home as part of a larger landscape of non-human diversity.

Looking over my shoulder, Piglet made a face. "That's depressing, isn't it? Don't you have any hope for the future? If you Large Creatures lose hope, we Small Animals are truly lost! You are our protectors and nurturers."

"I still have hope, Piglet, but hope comes from looking life square in the face in its wonder and tragedy. Nature is constantly renewing itself and will outlast human greed and foolishness. But, my hope is that we can wake up before it's too late. My hope is that I can wake up, and figure out what I need to do to make a difference. We can't leave it to politicians and their bullying, tweets, misinformation, and bloviating. When I think of these large institutions, sometimes I feel like a Small Animal too, and don't think I can make a difference. You have inspired me, Piglet, to be courageous despite my fears. I am afraid, Piglet, but in facing my fears I may find a way out for myself and those I love. Small is beautiful, and powerful, too, and from small actions great changes can begin."

"I know you won't give up," Piglet assured me. "It's not about you alone. It's about us. It's about your two little grandsons and kids everywhere. It's about all those children whose imaginations can flourish only if we care enough to face our fears with great love and hope. That's what I do."

The Wood will outlast the world-destroyers. Love will trump hate. Seeds of love will burst forth in world-weary hearts. But we need to be on the move, moving together to bring beauty to the earth and protection to the small and vulnerable. We adults need to reclaim enchantment; we need to remember days in which a child and his dog or stuffed toys awakened us to wonder everywhere and when anything was possible if you have a big enough imagination.

The Wood will always live deep in our hearts for as the final words of the Winnie the Pooh books note: "So they went off together. But wherever they go and whatever happens to them on the way, in that enchanted place on the top of the Forest, a little boy and his Bear will always be playing."[16]

"I hope you don't feel left out, Piglet that we ended with Christopher Robin and Pooh holding hands. For some children, you're the special friend and you're the one that reminds us of that special place in each of us where love abounds and life is fresh. I love Pooh, but you were always my favorite. Whenever I think of you, I think of all the little creatures that depend on us and the love that joins us regardless of time or place."

"No, I'm never left out. Wherever he goes, I'm in Pooh's heart and wherever I go Pooh's in mine, and we're always walking home together. God and all of us walking home together and discovering that our home is with God on each step on the journey. I think that's what process theology's all about, don't you?"

---

16 Ibid., 362.

Bruce Epperly is Pastor of South Congregational Church, United Church of Christ, Centerville, Massachusetts, and a member of the Doctor of Ministry faculty at Wesley Theological Seminary in Washington DC. He is the author of over fifty books, including *Process Theology: Embracing Adventure with God; Finding God in Suffering: A Journey with Job; Angels, Mysteries, and Miracles: A Progressive Vision;* and *The Gospel According to Winnie the Pooh*. His own 100 Aker Wood is the Cape Cod shoreline, where he walks daily, often with his grandchildren and playful Golden Doodle.

ABOUT PIGLET'S PROCESS

The prophet Isaiah once said "a little child will lead them." But, what about a character from Winnie the Pooh? Can anxious, yet adventurous, Piglet help us understand our relationship with God and one another? Theology is serious business. So serious that it can't be left solely to adults! Bruce Epperly's imaginative conversations with Piglet explore the contours of theological reflection from the perspective of Process Theology. Process Theology is often seen as far too complicated for adults to understand and impossible to teach or preach to laypeople. In this text, an experienced pastor and professor and a beloved character from the Winnie the Pooh stories bring Process Theology to life and explore themes such as beauty, spirituality, adventure, friendship, healing, and God's presence in our lives. In the spirit of Jesus' parables, *Piglet's Process* will inspire your imagination and creativity and invite you on an never-ending spiritual journey with a theologian, stuffed animal, and the healer from Nazareth as your companions.

Also from Energion Publications by Bruce Epperly

Topical Line Drives (https://topicallinedrives.com)

From Here to Eternity	$5.99
Jonah: When God Changes	$5.99
Process Theology: Embracing Adventure with God	$5.99
Process and Pastoral Care	$5.99
Process and Ministry	$5.99
Process Theology and Celtic Wisdom	$5.99
Process Spirituality	$5.99
One World: The Lord's Prayer from a Process Perspective	$5.99
The Energy of Love: Reiki and Christian Healing	$5.99
Ruth and Esther: Women of Agency and Adventure	$5.99

Participatory Study Guides (https://deepbiblestudy.com)

Galatians: A Participatory Study Guide	$12.99
Philippians: A Participatory Study Guide	$12.99

Other Titles (https://energiondirect.com/bruce-epperly)

Angels, Mysteries, and Miracles	$9.99
Transforming Acts	$14.99
Spiritual Decluttering:	
40 Days to Spiritual Transformation and Planetary Healing	$12.99
Finding God in Suffering: A Journey with Job	$9.99
Healing Marks	$14.99

Generous Quantity Discounts Available
Dealer Inquiries Welcome
Energion Publications — P.O. Box 841
Gonzalez, FL_ 32560
Website: http://energionpubs.com

www.ingramcontent.com/pod-product-compliance
Lightning Source LLC
LaVergne TN
LVHW011214080426
835508LV00007B/776